BEELEIGH ABBEY

a guide and history

CFP

Beeleigh Abbey
published by
Christopher Foyle Publishing Ltd
113-119 Charing Cross Road
London WC2H 0EB
June 2012

ISBN 978-0-9548896-2-3

To Catherine,
my loving partner and supporter in this and all our endeavours

CONTENTS

Aerial view of the site of Beeleigh Abbey close by the banks of the River Chelmer

FOREWORD

My grandfather William Foyle bought Beeleigh Abbey in the year of my birth, 1943. I stayed there often, first with my parents, and then as a boy and teenager with my cousins during school holidays. My grandparents were wonderful hosts. William had a great sense of fun, full of practical jokes, which he would spring on us and other guests. He would delight in showing and sharing with us the many rare medieval manuscripts in the library, with firing up the Bassett-Lowke steam trains and running them on the track in the attic, playing croquet and bowls on the lawn in the afternoons, and taking us fishing to the nearby rivers and canals – he never caught anything. Being president of the Maldon Angling Society, this caught the attention of Bing Crosby who broadcast a humorous skit about this on his radio programme in the United States. There were three square meals a day, served punctually at nine, one and seven thirty, as well as afternoon tea, and woe betide any guest who turned up late. Dinner was usually accompanied by Chateauneuf du Pape, followed by madeira, brandy, Benedictine, cigars and a game of cards. However, overriding everything was the love of the sheer antiquity of the building - its stones and its history.

ABOVE
Coat of arms and badge granted to Christopher Foyle by Garter King of Arms, Sir Conrad Swan, in 1994

I am sure that my grandfather would approve of this opportunity to welcome and guide others through the history of the house, its interior and its owners.

Christopher Foyle

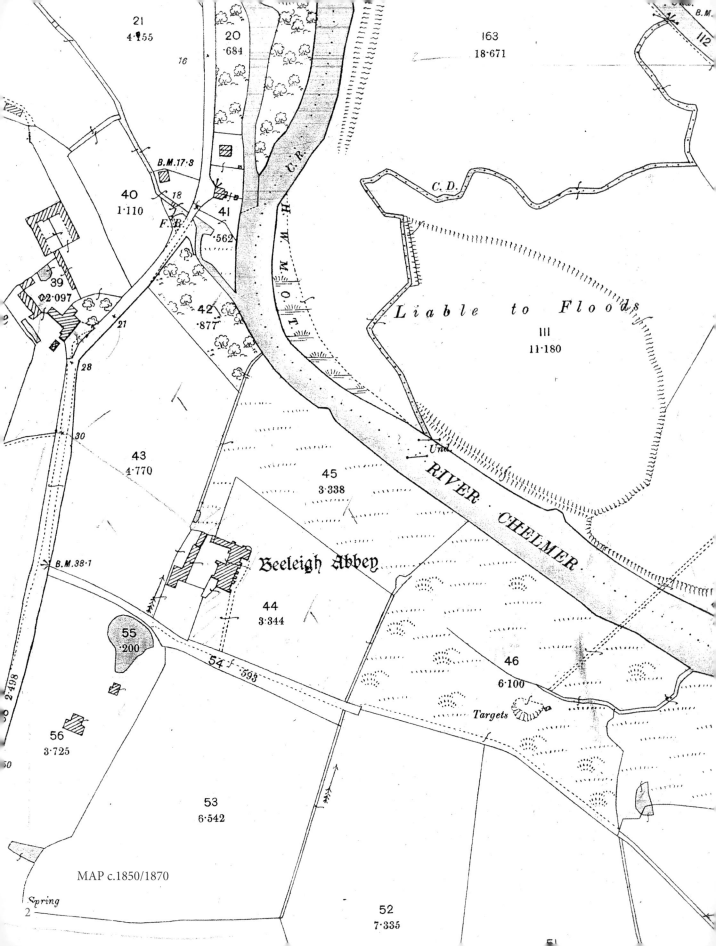

MAP c.1850/1870

Close by the banks of the upper tidal reaches of the River Chelmer, as it flows onwards to the Blackwater and the sea, less than a mile upstream from Maldon, stands Beeleigh Abbey, one of the most ancient continuously inhabited buildings in England.

Beeleigh Abbey today is what remains of the Premonstratensian monastery founded in 1180.

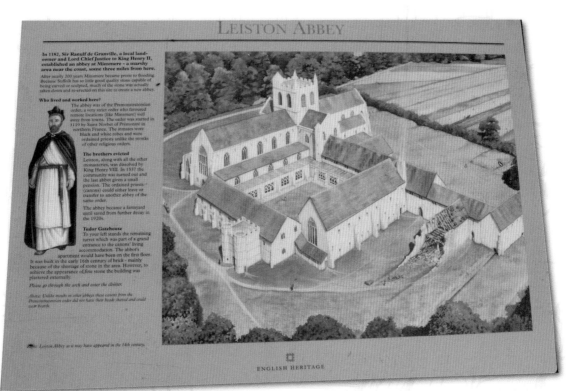

English Heritage interpretation of Leiston Abbey, very similar to Beeleigh Abbey

THE PREMONSTRATENSIAN ORDER

Beeleigh Abbey belonged to the Order of Premonstratensian or White Canons. Canons regular differed from secular canons in living together under rule and observing the statutes of their Orders, thus practically resembling monks, although they were never called monks, and their rule was not so strict. Canons were by definition priests and, unlike many monks, were not prohibited from serving parish churches, or constrained by the rigid rules of monastic seclusion. They spent time in the community looking after the spiritual well-being of lay people. They are generally considered to have been first instituted by Chrodegang, Bishop of Metz, c.760.

S. NORBERTUS
FUNDATOR ORD. PRAEM.

The founder of the Premonstratensian Order was St Norbert, which is why these canons were sometimes also called Norbertines. Norbert of Xanten was born in 1080 at Xanten in the Duchy of Cleves. His father was Herebert, Count of Gennep, who may have been a kinsman of the German emperor, Henry IV (1056-1105), while his mother Hawise or Hedwig of Guise was related to the Duke of Lorraine. Educated in the household of Archbishop Frederick of Cologne, he received a canonry and was ordained sub-deacon, but spent some years at the court of the Emperor Henry V. He was reputed, initially, to have lived a dissolute life.

However, one day in 1115, near Werden in Westphalia, when riding, he was overtaken by a sudden storm. As he looked for shelter, a ball of fire exploded at his horse's feet, burned up the grass and sank deep in the earth. On recovering his senses, he was struck with dismay when he thought about what might have happened to him in the next world, had he perished in his wickedness.

He decided to forsake his evil ways and began to prepare himself seriously for the life of a priest, selling his possessions, and giving his money to the poor. Then, clothed in a lamb-skin, with a hempen cord round his loins, he set out to preach repentance and a new life.

After preaching for several years through the northern provinces of France, he assembled around him those who wished to adopt his severe discipline. Seeing the salvation of so many committed to his care, he humbly prayed for divine direction; and thereupon the Blessed Virgin appeared to him in a vision. She pointed out to him a barren and lonesome spot in the valley of Coucy, thereafter called Pré-montré.

In 1119 at Rheims he obtained the approval of Pope Calixtus II to found a new monastic order. The Bishop of Laon invited him to his diocese, and St Bernard of Clairvaux offered a site in the Forest of St Gobain, ten miles from Laon, presumably the location that was pointed out to him in his vision. It was here, on Christmas Day 1121, that Norbert and forty others founded the first house of his new Order. Norbert was later created Archbishop of Magdeburg and, after an active and laborious ministry, died in 1134.

One of the products of the religious reform movements of the 12th century, the Premonstratensians adopted the rule of St Augustine of Hippo, as used by the Augustinian Canons, but with some modifications. Probably influenced by St Bernard, the new Order was somewhat like the Cistercians in its austere lifestyle and organisation and choice of isolated sites for their houses. These were laid out with considerable attention paid to the management of local resources in order to provide fresh water for drinking and washing, and to feed the fishponds and drain the latrines. Unlike the Augustinian houses, which were generally independent of each other, the Premonstratensians had a system of affiliation and dependence, the Abbot of Prémontré being in overall charge, as a result of which the Order was exempt from episcopal control.

A White Canon of St Norbert (described by some as St Norbert himself) attributed to Hans Memling 1435 - 1494 in the Antwerp Museum

Each house of men was governed by an abbot. Their dress was white, with white rochet and white cap, as a result of which they were known as the White Canons, as distinct from the Augustinians who wore black.

The Premonstratensians were one of the most successful of the new orders to emerge out of the ferment that swept through Europe in the 11th and 12th centuries. The Order achieved a phenomenal expansion during the following 130 years, establishing a network of houses extending from Ireland to Palestine and from Scandinavia and the Baltic to Spain and Italy.

There were thirty four houses of the Premonstratensian Order in England, including two nunneries.

The first Premonstratensian foundation in this country was at Newham, "Newhouse", in Lincolnshire, which was colonised in 1143 from Licques, near Calais, a daughter house of Prémontré, and from which all the English houses, except St Radegund's in Kent and Bayham in Sussex, were descended. Beeleigh was one such daughter of Newhouse, but was afterwards treated as the responsibility of the little abbey of Durford in Sussex. Beeleigh was the only Premonstratensian Abbey in Essex, its nearest neighbours being Leiston in Suffolk, and Langdon and St Radegund's in Kent.

RIGHT
St Norbert preaching to the people of Antwerp.

J Brueghel the Elder 1568 - 1625. In the James I bedroom at Beeleigh Abbey

BEELEIGH ABBEY

THE HISTORY OF THE ABBEY

Foundation

Ralph, Abbot of Coggeshall, states in his Chronicle that in 1180, the canons of Parndon (a locality now occupied by part of Harlow New Town) migrated to Maldon. Nothing more is known, however, of this earlier settlement beyond the names of donors of land, and the occurrence of Robert, Abbot of "Perhendune", in August 1172 as a witness to a charter of Ralph de Marci to Colchester Abbey.

The new site at Maldon was granted by Robert Mantell, Lord of the Manor of Little Maldon, who had been Sheriff of Essex in 1170. His gifts were so generous that he was considered the founder of the abbey. Besides the site for the construction of the abbey, Robert Mantell provided the new inhabitants with two islands and the right of patronage over three parochial churches. Ralph of Lagefare, Bulcelina of Langford, and Ralph of Marcil further enriched the abbey with grants of land. The patronage of the abbey passed through Robert Mantell's sons, Matthew and Robert, to his successors as lords of the manor. By the marriage of Lucy Mantell, younger daughter of the younger Robert, it came to the Fillol family, and from Thomas Fillol it passed to John de Grey and from him to John Amory, who held it in 1320. In 1365 it belonged to John de Bourchier and it remained with the Bourchier family until the dissolution.

BELOW
Statue of Robert Mantell in the gardens at Beeleigh Abbey

On 7th December 1189 Richard I granted to the abbey a charter of confirmation of lands and liberties (including the parish churches of All Saints and St Peter, Maldon), which was afterwards confirmed by Edward III in 1364. At first the abbey was referred to as the "Abbey and Convent of Maldon" and was not called Beeleigh until the 13th century when the names "Belegh" and "Bilege" first appear. The abbey church was dedicated to St Nicholas, but later the Blessed Virgin Mary (St Mary) shared the dedication.

The canons built their abbey on ground rising above the level of the River Chelmer, about three quarters of a mile outside of the town of Maldon. It is probable that they constructed the church first. The earliest buildings for habitation and study may have been wooden. More substantial stone structures were finally completed about 1220.

During the next sixty years we know nothing of the history of the abbey beyond some names of abbots and some acquisitions of lands.

Abbots of Beeleigh

1172	Robert (abbot of Parndon)
1188	Henry
1209	Henry
1235	Henry
1247 - 1249	John
1253 - 1254	Walter
1254 - 1262	Roger
1265	Andrew
1268 - 1269	Reginald
1272 - 1280	Andrew
1298	R
1323	William de Rokelaunde
1323 - 1331	William Compton
-	Richard de Purleee
1373	William
1384	John
1384 - 1405	Thomas Cokke
1404 - 1427	John Colchestre
1429 - 1439	Stephen Manweden
1439 - 1443	Thomas Ormesby (?)
1440 - 1461	John Boston
1462 - 1478	William Kirkeby
1481 - 1509	Thomas Skarlet
1513 - 1536	John Copsheffe

Estate and income

Beeleigh Abbey was built, and the canons maintained and other expenses met, largely through the income generated from its landed estate. Although there is no surviving cartulary or collection of records, details of the abbey's endowments were recorded in royal charters of Henry II and Richard I and in valuations of its temporalities in 1291 and 1535. Further evidence is available from documents produced for the Crown at the time of the dissolution.

The original lands granted to the community in Parndon later formed the manor of Canons in Great Parndon and remained in the hands of the abbey. They were greatly augmented, however, by Robert Mantell's gifts at Beeleigh and Maldon and the surrounding district that included lands, for example, at Totham and Goldhanger. Robert and his wife also gave the abbey four churches including All Saints and St Peter in Maldon, a house in that town and another in London.

Later gifts and purchases from the 12th to the 15th century extended the abbey's estate in both Maldon and Parndon, and also across other Essex parishes to include valuable holdings in Purleigh, Goldhanger, Woodham Mortimer, Burnham-on-Crouch, and Tollesbury. The abbey also acquired the advowsons, rectories and tithes of the churches of Great Wakering and Ulting. In 1481 the abbey appropriated under licence the decayed hospital of St Giles in Maldon, and the canons thereafter undertook all the financial and religious responsibilities of the hospital.

Early image of Beeleigh Abbey: Drawing c 1705 by William Stukeley (Bodleian Library). Showing north and south ends which, by the 19th century, had disappeared

The East Prospect of Belygs Abby near Maldon Essex.

By the time of the dissolution the estate's demesne (the land held and managed directly by the abbey) comprised over 400 acres, of which about three quarters was leased to tenants and one quarter retained as a 'home farm'. The latter appears to have remained intact under the estate's later lay owners as the home farm at Beeleigh, measured at 107 acres in 1759.

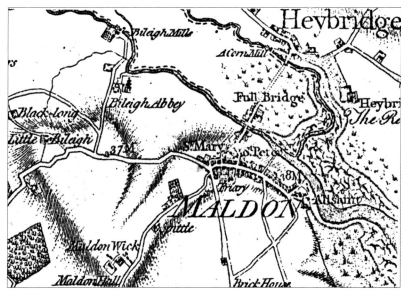

Beyond the demesne were further landholdings and economic assets of different types. There were a number of customary tenants, whose tenancies had descended from the unfree peasants of the Middle Ages. They held their lands by copy of the entry on the court roll recording their admittance into their holding, and hence were called copyholders. Their rents were low, having become fixed by custom in the Middle Ages, but they paid a large 'entry fine' when holdings were transferred on death or sale.

Beeleigh Abbey and the surrounding district. From the Chapman and André survey of 1777.

LEFT
The abbey 1819
by Charles Warren

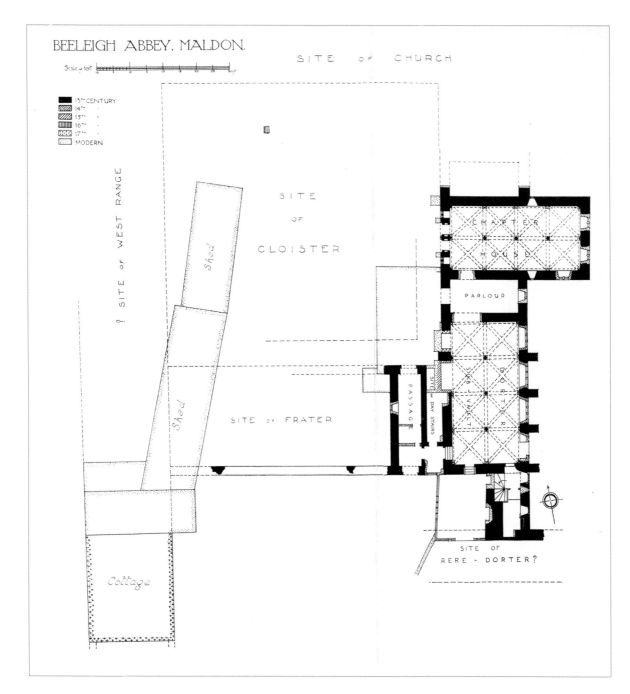

ABOVE
Plan of Beeleigh Abbey today; also showing the outline of previous buildings dismantled.

A more significant larger body were freeholders who held their land by charter, fealty, suit of court and an annual rent in money. These included the holders of many tenements and messuages in the town of Maldon, the tenants of the rectories of Great Wakering and Ulting, and the demesne sub-tenancies of the manors of Hazeleigh Hall and Ulting Hall where Beeleigh abbey was the feudal overlord. The lords of Ulting Hall and Hazeleigh Hall still paid their quit rents to the Beeleigh manor in 1813. Some of the freehold tenancies in 1528 were large and valuable to the abbey: for example, the rectories of Ulting and Wakering. The tenement and dairy farm known as "Collewards" in Burnham Marsh, leased to two farmers from Althorne, could be stocked with 24 cows and 240 sheep.

One immediately post-dissolution document reveals that the estate produced an income, including leases and tithes, totalling £79. 9s. 3¾d. The manor of Canons in Great Parndon alone produced £13. 2s. 7d., its lands probably including both the original endowment and additional gifts in that parish. Later, in 1546, that manor was separated from Beeleigh by the Crown and granted to Sir Thomas Darcy. Other 16th century documents reveal the abbey's ownership of a dye-house in Maldon, of a stall or shop in the town's market-place, and tenements occupied by two inns, the Chequers and the Whitehart. At Goldhanger the estate owned 'weirs', a local form of fish-trap that was commonplace along the Blackwater estuary. The abbey also owned a tenement, once called le Crane and later le Greyhounde, at St Mary Axe, Aldgate, in the parish of St Andrew Undershaft, which may have originally served as the abbey's London town house.

The abbey. Published by Longman, Hurst *et al* 1 January 1815

Beeleigh's famous son

St Roger Niger de Biliye, as he was known, was an important character in the history of the English Church in the 13th century and, following his death in 1241, the object of a flourishing cult based at Beeleigh.

At about the time that Beeleigh Abbey was founded, a baby boy was born to a couple named Ralph and Margery. His name was Roger and in contemporary medieval documents he is referred to variously as Roger "Niger", "Le Noir", "The Blacke", "de Biliye", or "de Byleie". The early surname 'Niger' usually refers to the complexion of skin or to the colour of hair. However, Roger had a younger brother, Walter, Canon of St Paul's, who is also recorded as "Niger", which suggests that he inherited an existing family surname from his father. However, "de Biliye" denotes an association with Beeleigh, either because he lived there, or because his parents entrusted him to the canons to educate him and prepare him for a career in the Church, or both.

In 1192 Roger was in residence at St Paul's in London where he was a prebendary of "Ealdland", land in Tillingham that provided him with an income. By 1218 he had secured further ecclesiastical preferment, becoming Archdeacon of Colchester. The Archdeaconry also had its administrative base at St Paul's and a corresponding seat within the cathedral.

The abbey 1818. Engraved by J Craig from a drawing by J Allen for 'Excursions through Essex'

When Eustace de Fauconberge, Bishop of London, died in 1228, the Dean and Chapter of St Paul's chose Roger as his successor. His consecration took place at Canterbury on 10th June 1229. According to the contemporary St Alban's monk and chronicler, Matthew Paris, Roger was "… a very reverend man, religious, learned, painful in preaching, eloquent, a great house-keeper, of very courteous and gentle behaviour…".

As well as secular and administrative responsibilities, Roger played a leading role in the conduct of services in the cathedral. On 20th January 1230, an important date in that it was the anniversary of the conversion of St Paul, Roger was taking high mass when there then came, in the words of Matthew Paris,

The Consecration of Archbishop Edmond of Canterbury by Roger Niger, Bishop of London (right). Drawn by Matthew Paris in the margin of the Historia Anglorum © The British Library Board. Royal MS 14c vii

"a sudden darkness (which) overshadowed the choir and therewith came such a tempest of thunder and lightning that the people there assembled thought verily the church and steeple had come down on their heads". If this was not frightening enough, there then followed "… such a filthy savor and stink that partly for fear that they might not abide the savor, they avoided the church falling on heaps on one another as they sought to get out of the same".

The priests and canons forsook their desks, but Bishop Roger was unmoved and, assisted by one remaining deacon, calmly finished the service. Afterwards, when the air began to clear, the people returned into the church and were humbled by the sight of the Bishop who, it was recorded, "remained undaunted".

Roger was actively involved in affairs of church and state. He defended the rights of the church against Henry III, incurring the king's displeasure. He also found himself out of favour with the Pope and was summoned to Rome to answer for his actions, being robbed of his money and jewels in Parma on the way. He was prominent at major events, such as the consecration of Edmund Archbishop Canterbury in 1234, the coronation of Queen Eleanor of Provence in 1236 at Westminster Abbey, and the baptism of her son, the future King Edward I, in 1239.

Roger left his mark on old St Paul's, the medieval cathedral that preceded the existing one. In the words of the 17th century antiquarian, Sir William Dugdale, "that this Roger was a great benefactor to the … fabric cannot be doubted …".

Work undertaken during Roger's incumbency reached its culmination with the consecration of a new choir in 1240. Those who attended included King Henry III, Edmond Archbishop of Canterbury, Otto the Pope's legate, six other bishops and many nobles and magnates. The occasion was felt to be so important that Roger procured "An indulgence of forty days pardon (or forgiveness) to all those (people who were there and) … agreed to truly confess of their sins".

In failing health, Roger retired to Bishop's Hall in the parish of Stepney and died there just twelve months after completing his work at St Paul's on Michaelmas Day (the Feast of St Michael), 29th September 1241. His body was taken to St Paul's Cathedral, where it was buried at 3 o'clock in the afternoon. At that precise moment, and to the amazement of all those gathered, an eclipse of the sun occurred.

Roger's last resting place, prior to the Great Fire of 1666, was between the north aisle and the beautiful choir that had been so special to him during his life on earth, standing between the fifth and sixth pillars (from the west) of the choir and touching the fifth pillar. An engraving of his tomb is shown in Dugdale's 'History of St Paul's' (1658).

The tomb was soon seen as a "special place". Matthew Paris tells us that "many miracles were wrought at the tomb of Roger", that there were "wonderful events" and that the place "shone forth with remarkable (happenings)". Then, in 1249, Roger is referred to in a manuscript as "Sanctus" – St Roger.

Roger's tomb in St Paul's Cathedral prior to the Great Fire of 1666. From W Dugdale's 'History' of 1658

By the 13th century canonisation was a solemn judgement reserved by canon law to the Pope. Roger's canonisation was never formally requested from the Holy See and he was thus one of the number of notable medieval people for whom a popular local cult was established but never officially recognised. There are other similar examples, such as of Robert of Abingdon, Simon of Sudbury and Simon de Montfort.

Roger's 'saintly status' ensured a constant stream of pilgrims determined to see the tomb, to pray, to hope for a miracle and leave their dues. Indulgences were granted to those who visited the tomb; it became a major attraction, yielding substantial income for the cathedral. Items connected with Roger such as a large cushion, as well as his red silk ecclesiastical cope with a hood and with stars and roses on it, were treasured as relics. At Hatfield Broadoak Priory in Essex, a large gold episcopal ring, which once belonged to 'St Roger of Byleye', was jealously guarded.

Another much more unusual object found its way to St Roger's native and beloved Beeleigh Abbey. There is evidence that St Roger's heart was removed before his internment in St Paul's and was sent to Beeleigh Abbey as a holy relic. In the regnal year 1248-1249, the Abbot of Maldon (i.e. Beeleigh) agreed that he and his successors would "… find and maintain one cereum (wax candle) to burn every day at the mass of the Blessed Virgin Mary and at the great mass of the high altar in the church of Maldon before the heart of St Roger for ever …". Furthermore, Pope Boniface IX, on 22nd July 1391, granted relaxation of six years and six quadragene (the forty days of Lent) to penitents who on the feast of St Roger (29th September) should visit Beeleigh and give alms to the church of the monastery.

There are many other examples of 'heart burials', such as Richard the Lionheart, and Richard Poore, Bishop of Chichester, Salisbury and Durham, who on his death in 1232 had his body interred at Chichester and his heart at Tarrant, Dorset, where he was born.

Roger's heart was probably housed in a shrine, or richly gilded and decorated casket. Many pilgrims would have visited the abbey and donated the obligatory gifts that would have generated considerable income for the abbey.

It was probably for this reason that King Edward I and Queen Eleanor visited the abbey in 1289, having made visits of devotion to the shrines of many other saints starting with that of St Thomas Becket of Canterbury.

There is no evidence as to what happened to St Roger's shrine or casket when all religious houses were suppressed in the dissolution ordered by Henry VIII from 1536. There was no general act dealing with the disposal of shrines and relics, although the king made it clear that "… the images and bones of such as (the people) restored and offered up to with ornaments of the same (should) be taken away…". The destruction of shrines was carried out by the local commissioners responsible for the general closure of an abbey or priory. Their aim was to prevent any such item from becoming the object of a "renewed superstition and veneration".

The commissioners, Sir John St Clere, Humphrey Brown, Sergeant of Law, Francis Jobson and Thomas Mildmay, arrived at Beeleigh and an inventory was taken on 6th June 1536. Rather curiously, it appears to have been only partly completed as there are obvious omissions and a complete section of the inventory was kept separate and delivered to the abbot because he was to remain responsible for "certain parcels of goods and chattels….". The inventory included items found in the abbey church, not least "a table of alabaster at the High Alter…", its reredos, hangings, brass and gilt copper cross and candlesticks, but there is no mention of any associated shrine, casket relic, or anything else loosely associated with St Roger.

Perhaps the shrine was destroyed, but there is a persistent local tradition that shortly before the commissioners arrived, the object was spirited away by the canons and secretly concealed in a place known only to them. Exactly the same was said to have happened at Durham where the remains of St Cuthbert were allegedly recovered and hidden by the Benedictine monks. The shrine of St Roger has not been seen or heard of since.

A royal visit

As previously mentioned, the only recorded visit of an English sovereign to Beeleigh occurred in 1289. King Edward I was present on 9th September and Queen Eleanor on 10th September when masses were celebrated in the abbey for the soul of Hugh Fitz Otho, the king's steward who had been a benefactor of the house. They gave three shillings and eight pence in alms offering and seven shillings and six pence for pittance for the abbot and convent. The king dated letters patent at Beeleigh on 10th September.

The abbot is poisoned

Other grants followed and the future of the abbey seemed secure. Life at Beeleigh continued without major incident until the appointment of a new abbot, Thomas Cokke, in October 1384. In 1392 he obtained the dignity of papal chaplain from Pope Boniface IX.

However, in the winter of 1403-4 he became involved, as were also the Abbot of Colchester and the Prior of St Osyth, in the conspiracy of the Countess of Oxford and others against Henry IV, fuelled by the rumour that Richard II was still alive. A warrant for his arrest was issued on 5th June and he surrendered. On 22nd June at Great Codham Hall, Wethersfield, the residence of Sir William Coggeshall, he made a detailed confession. A commission was appointed in August to investigate the conspiracy, and the abbot was probably found guilty on some charges, but as a result of the queen's intervention he received a pardon on 13th November.

He did not, however, survive long. An inquisition taken before the sheriff and one of the coroners of Surrey on 24th July 1405 found that John Ultyng, a fellow canon of Thomas Cokke, late Abbot of Beeleigh, on Friday next after the Feast of the Annunciation of St Mary in that year, poisoned the said Thomas Cokke, his abbot, at Southwark, from which the same Thomas Cokke languished for eleven weeks and then died. A warrant for Ultyng's arrest was issued on 29th July, but it is possible that he cleared himself of the charge, for a canon of Beeleigh of the same name later became abbot of Durford in the following January.

On 28th June 1930, to commemorate the 750th anniversary of the abbey, the Essex County Drama Society re-enacted Abbot Cokke being taken ill.

A famous patron

The most distinguished of the patrons of the abbey was Henry Bourchier, who was created Viscount Bourchier about 1446, appointed treasurer in 1455-6 under Henry VI and in 1461-2 under Edward IV, and created Earl of Essex in 1461. He died on 4th April 1483 and he and his wife, Isabel, sister of Richard, Duke of York, father of Edward IV, who died on 2nd October 1484, were buried in the chapel of St Mary in the abbey church.

Sir John Bourchier, son of Henry Bourchier, by his will, proved 1495, left his body to be buried near his parents and instructed that a tomb be made there for him, and for both of his wives. In the event, he was buried at Stebbing but his widow, Dame Elizabeth Bourchier, by her will, proved 14 May 1498, left her body to be buried in the chapel of St Mary in the abbey church and that the bones of her husband be removed from Stebbing and carried to join her in the tomb. When the Bourchiers failed to acquire the abbey at the dissolution, they had their tombs in this chapel, which was effectively a family mausoleum, moved to Little Easton church near Dunmow where the brass to the first earl can still be seen.

ABOVE
Brass rubbing of the tombs of Henry Bourchier, first Earl of Essex, and his wife Isabel Plantagenet, moved from the chapel at Beeleigh Abbey to Little Easton church, near Dunmow

Inspections

From the later 14th century, the English Premonstratensian houses were under the control of a commissary-general who represented the abbot of Premontré. The commissary-general from 1458 to 1505 was Richard Redman, Abbot of Shap, and later Bishop of St Asaph and finally of Ely. Records of the visitations or inspections of the English houses by Redman during his long tenure of office are preserved in the Bodleian and other libraries, and give a fascinating and unique insight into the lives of these monastic communities. He visited Beeleigh several times and his reports are exceptionally favourable, revealing it to have been one of the better run abbeys with a high standard of observance of the rule.

ABOVE
Tomb of Bishop Redman at Ely Cathedral.
By permission of Ely Cathedral

On one of his visitations to Beeleigh on 25th August 1482, it is recorded that Thomas Lambe was ordered to say the whole psalter within forty days for striking one of his brethren. Nicholas Brige was sentenced to one day on bread and water for disobedience and for breaking silence in the cloister. Nothing else had to be reformed and all things spiritual and temporal were in good order under the new abbot, Thomas Skarlett. All the canons were to observe a higher standard of tonsure, and an order was given that all those going out of the dormitory without licence after compline, the last service of the day, were to be put on bread and water for three days. The debt of the house was shown as £100. 16s. as against 20 marks (£13. 6s. 8d) at the last visitation, chiefly on account of expenses arising probably from the dilapidated condition of the buildings. There were ten canons, two of whom were novices.

On 8th July 1488, the bishop recorded that nothing was found worthy of reformation and all things were being done to the glory of God, through the prudent rule of the abbot. He saw, however, with his own eyes, carelessness as to tonsure and considered it was not decent to have such an abundance of hair. The debt was then reduced to £76 and there was enough cattle, grain, and farm produce. The canons numbered thirteen, four being novices. At the next visitation, on 3rd October 1491, everything was in commendably good order, the debt had been cleared off, and the abbey was well stocked with grain and livestock.

Redman visited again on 9th October 1497 when Thomas Skarlett was still abbot and there were twelve canons including three novices. This time Redman found nothing wrong, no debt and plenty of grain and animals.

On 9th October 1500, the bishop saw and praised the very beautiful buildings of the church and its excellent new windows, and although these were costly, there was no debt, the house being well supplied with grain and cattle.

Typically, these visitations indicate that the population of the abbey consisted of the abbot, the sub prior, and between seven and twelve canons, including novices. By the time of the dissolution, and probably from the early 1500s, there may have been only six to nine canons in residence, living comfortably, and the life of the abbey was more like that of a small Cambridge college than a monastery.

	Principal patrons during the monastic period
1180 - 1190	Robert Mantell
1190 - c.1214	Matthew Mantell (son of the above)
c.1214 - 1228	Robert Mantell II (brother of the above)
1228 - before 1250	Matthew Mantell II (son of the above)
- 1289	Cecily Mantell (widow of the above)
1365 -	John de Bourchier
- 1483	Henry Bourchier 1st Earl of Essex
- 1484	Isobel, Countess of Essex,(sister of Richard, Duke of York who was father of Edward IV)
- 1495	Sir John Bourchier (4th son of the above)
- 1498	Dame Elizabeth Bourchier
- 1498	Lady Mary Nevile
- 1536	Henry Bourchier 2nd Earl of Essex (grandson of the 1st Earl)

The Dissolution

In 1536, the yearly value of the abbey was £157.16s.11¼d. so, being less than £200, it came under the Act for the Dissolution of the smaller religious houses. The last abbot, John Copsheffe, received a pension of £18 per annum and was allowed to retain the vicarage of Ulting until his resignation in 1545, on his acceptance of the royal supremacy of the Church. Having conformed to the new religion, he retained his vicarage, unlike some abbots who did not succumb to the authority of the monarch in breaking with Rome.

The patron at the time of the dissolution was Henry Bourchier, second Earl of Essex, who had inherited the title on the death of his grandfather in 1483. Bourchier was a member of Henry VII's Privy Council and was present at the siege of Boulogne in 1492. He was created a Knight of the Garter in 1496. When Henry VIII became king, he was made captain of the new bodyguard, and in 1513 was lieutenant-general of the spears at the sieges of Therouanne and Tournai. The following year he was made chief captain of the king's forces, and in 1520 he bore the Sword of State at the Field of the Cloth of Gold.

Portrait of Henry Bourchier, second Earl of Essex from 'Memoirs of the Court of Queen Elizabeth' published in 1825/Bridgeman Art Library

Interestingly, he had written to Thomas Cromwell, Henry VIII's chief minister, in 1532, "two children at my own cost in the house of the canons of Bylegh, of which I am founder and someone has come from King's College, Cambridge, with a placard to take them from me. I want a placard to keep them still, or the services of God cannot be maintained". The earl was, of course, having the children educated to become canons who should devote themselves to the welfare of his soul and of those of his ancestors.

In a letter to Thomas Cromwell, on 13th January 1536, the earl wrote: "And I thancke you of your goodnes shewyd unto the abbot of Beyle prayeng you to contynew your goodnes unto hym". We do not know what is meant by this. An inventory of the goods and cattle was taken on 6th June and this effectively marks the end of the monastery. The comment by the Earl of Essex to Cromwell, coupled with the fact that some of the rooms of the house were omitted and that there was very little of value shown in the inventory, is interesting. Could it be that items of significant value were kept by the abbot or others and not handed over to the king's commissioners? If so, could this have given rise to persistent rumours in the 16th century of buried treasure at Beeleigh Abbey? More of this later.

ABOVE
Three images of the abbey 1818
by Draper, engraved by R B Peake

The Earl of Essex hoped to obtain the abbey and wrote to Cromwell with that idea on 23 March 1536:

"My right single good master in my most hearty manner, I heartily recommend me unto you trusting in your goodness to put the King in remembrance in as much as the act is passed that all places of religion being under three hundred marks be wholly in His Grace's hands among which the little house of Byleygh whereof I was founder lyeth entirely and whole within my land wherefore if it may please the King's grace to give it me as peaceably as it is his I shall give His Grace a thousand marks to be paid in three years trusting in your bounty and goodness and for the poor service that I have done His Highness by keeping it never to be house of religion hereafter and that little which I have and it shall always at your commandment and your pains so looked on that I trust ye shall be pleased. Written at my poor house of Benyngton this twenty third day of March".

The earl had earlier curried favour with Henry VIII by writing to the Pope in support of Henry's divorce from Catherine of Aragon and had acted in an official capacity at the coronation of Anne Boleyn. However, he was by now deaf, "except a man speak very loud even in my ear I may not hear a whit" as he told Cromwell, and he was decrepit. A contemporary described him as "an old man, of little whit and less experience, without power".

The abbey 1832.
A drawing by W Bartlett engraved by C Mottram

The earl was ignored in favour of the ambitious John Gates (or Gate) of Great Garnetts, High Easter, who came from an old Essex gentry family and was a member of the privy chamber of Henry VIII. Henry VIII had a 'fixer' in his court, Sir Anthony Denny. Henry became increasingly reliant on Sir Anthony and "he rapidly became the true authority lurking behind the throne". As the king's reliance on Denny grew, the courtier set up a small administrative unit within the Privy Chamber. It was led by John Gates, his brother-in-law. Gates was reputed to be "a bit of a thug and the original 16th century 'Essex' man, who was used as the hard man to get things done around the court". Denny and Gates effectively controlled the Privy Purse, Henry's private bank account, and for the last six years of Henry's reign, was entrusted with large sums of crown money. Denny and Gates "had no compunction in exploiting their unique access to the king with the many subjects who wished to press their suits". His services during the rebellion of 1536, when he was instructed to keep order in Essex, may have earned him the king's gratitude, for he soon became a royal confidant. He was also one of the most active agents of the dissolution. He arrested rioters in Essex and carried through the official destruction of "superstitious altars". He witnessed the king's will, under which he received £200, and he rode beside the king's corpse in the funeral procession at Windsor. He was captain of the guard to Edward VI, vice-chamberlain of his household, chancellor of the Duchy of Lancaster, a privy councillor and Sheriff of Essex in 1549.

John Gates obtained the lease of the abbey on 8th January 1537 and then proceeded to demolish those parts of it and its precincts that he did not require for his own use. On 15th July 1540, for a payment of £300 (about half its market value), he obtained a grant of the lordship and site of the monastery and certain possessions in the neighbourhood, including Beeleigh Mill and the rectories and advowsons of the churches of St Peter and All Saints, Maldon. The whole was valued at £35.10s.11½d. yearly at a rent of £3.11s.2d.

Gates made regular purchases of property, sometimes alone, sometimes in partnership, often to resell at a profit, occasionally to exchange. Together with royal grants, these transactions gave him wide estates in Essex and elsewhere worth in excess of £13,000. Gates disposed of Beeleigh Abbey in 1546.

Knighted at the coronation of Edward VI, Gates only obtained a strategic position at court under Edward VI after the overthrow of the Protector Somerset in 1549, when he became right hand man to the Duke of Northumberland. It was Gates whom Northumberland was to reproach as having been behind the plot to make Lady Jane Grey queen. As captain of the guard Gates played a leading role in the brief reign of Queen Jane. On 9th July 1553 he told his subordinates of the dead king's wishes that his cousin Jane Grey be proclaimed queen, and the next day he took possession of the Tower. On 14th July he followed Northumberland to Cambridge at the head of the household troops. From there it was believed that it was their intention to proceed against Princess Mary at Framlingham Castle and kill her. Meanwhile, however, news reached Cambridge that the Privy Council in London had done a U-turn, forsaken Jane and proclaimed Mary. Gates was arrested in Cambridge, together with Northumberland, in the small hours of 20th/21st July by his own royal guard, who had decided to change sides. Gates re-entered the Tower on 25th July as Mary's prisoner and remained there until 19th August, when he was tried and sentenced to death for treason. Three days later he was brought out to Tower Hill, "where at three blows his head was stricken off". He is, traditionally, one of a number of 'spirits' who are still said to inhabit the abbey!

Jean Boulanger (attributed)
Lady Jane Grey, Lana Graya
Engraving 17th century
The Fitzwilliam Museum, Cambridge

Buried treasure and secret tunnels

Fifty five years after the dissolution, in March 1591, a curious case went before the authorities at the Maldon Borough Sessions. Edmund Hunt, a Maldon innkeeper stood accused of contravening an earlier statute of 1563 that expressly directed "against Conjuracions, Inchantments and Witchecrafts". It was alleged that Hunt had been overheard talking with John Mace a queen's messenger and Thomas Badcock at the White Hart Inn at Fullbridge, Maldon, regarding treasures "hydd in the grownde… about Byelie". It was said that he even produced a crude map "wherin were wrytten manye crosses…" and previously via a third party called Thomas Collyne had a "peece of ye earth" from Beeleigh analysed by the renowned mystic, and great conjurer, astrologer and scientist of the age, Dr John Dee. It was decided that Hunt should be bound over in £20 and ordered to appear at the next Sessions, but the sequel to this story has not survived.

What was Hunt looking for? Why was he convinced to the very point of breaking the law that something precious was buried at Beeleigh? Was he searching for booty hidden by the canons? Did that treasure allegedly include an elusive gold and jewelled relic casket containing the heart of St Roger?

Thomas Wright in his 'Picturesque Beauties of Great Britain' published in 1834 states that:

"hidden treasure, stone coffins and human skeletons had been found beneath the ruins. There have been many rumours of hidden treasure at Beeleigh Abbey, going back to Elizabethan times, but history does not relate whether or when such treasure was ever actually found and what it consisted of. If treasure was ever found, then presumably those who found it would have kept very quiet".

There have also been persistent local legends, probably dating from this time, about a tunnel that extends from the abbey in various directions to Beeleigh Mill and even as far as All Saints Church!

LATER OWNERS

Thomas Franck was the owner at his death on 9th February 1580, when his son and heir Richard succeeded him. In his will Thomas Franck was described as being of the Rise, Hatfield Broad Oak. He was not resident at Beeleigh, which he had leased in 1559 to Roger Warfilde, Henry Kinge and Edmund More. It was during the ownership of Thomas Franck's son Richard that the three-storey timber-framed extension was built in 1624. Richard died on 28th October 1627 and Beeleigh then apparently passed not to his eldest son, Leventhorpe, but instead to his second son Richard.

It remained in the hands of the Franck (or Franke) family until 1633 when it passed from Sir Leventhorpe Franke, Lucy his wife and Richard Franke, gentleman, to Thomas Craythorne, gentleman who, according to the county historian Philip Morant, was one of the receivers in the Custom House, London. From John Craythorne, son of Thomas, and Ann his wife, it passed in 1653 to Robert Ingram, the estate still possessing the advowsons of the two united churches of All Saints and St Peter's. On his death, it descended to his son Richard Ingram of London, merchant, who mortgaged it on 21st October 1670 to Sir Arthur Ingram. The mortgage was afterwards paid off and the estate bought from Richard Ingram for £1,700 on 27th and 28th September 1698 by John Bludworth of London, merchant. The latter died in the following January, leaving his son John Bludworth his heir, but the elder John had settled it for her life on his wife Utritia, daughter of John Banks, who brought a Chancery Suit against the borough in 1702 to avoid payment of the tax called 'land cheap' on this purchase, claiming that Beeleigh was not within the limits of the borough. Utritia afterwards married the Rev Walter Stert, who was vicar of Conwood in Devonshire from 1715-1747.

The younger John Bludworth succeeded on her death and by his will dated 1734, proved on 22nd July 1737, various persons became entitled successively to the estate: Sarah Clifton who died in 1740, Thomas Snell who died in 1750, and John Fortescue MB who died in 1776. On his death several persons became entitled to possession under various wills and administrations either as trustees or as beneficial owners in a share of the property. In January 1778 they sold it to Abraham Shuttleworth of Maldon Hall and Benjamin Rosewell of London, and in 1801 it was settled on Frances Baker (née Shuttleworth) on her marriage to Benjamin Baker.

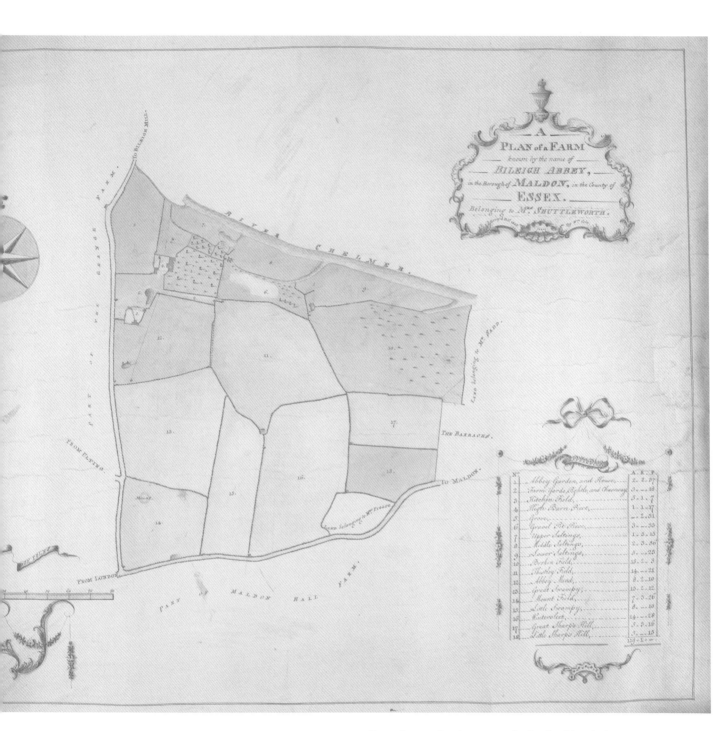

Farm known by the name of Bileigh Abbey belonging
to Mrs Shuttleworth survey'd by Wm Cole. 1805
Essex Record Office

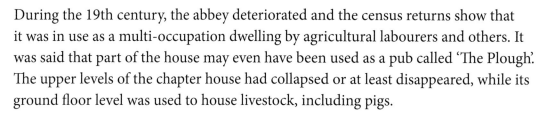

During the 19th century, the abbey deteriorated and the census returns show that it was in use as a multi-occupation dwelling by agricultural labourers and others. It was said that part of the house may even have been used as a pub called 'The Plough'. The upper levels of the chapter house had collapsed or at least disappeared, while its ground floor level was used to house livestock, including pigs.

John Doyle Field, a widower and retired engineer who formerly worked for the Indian Civil Service, lived at the abbey for twenty years from about 1891 and despite ill health he undertook extensive work in developing the gardens. This was noted at the time for its choice collection of English flowers, including arches of climbing roses. He also took a keen interest in the history of the building and encouraged archaeologists to view the place. The splendid bearded gentleman with a shock of white hair featured in photographs of the abbey and its grounds in the 1890s and early 1900s is probably John Doyle Field. He died aged 78 on 5th December 1911 and his grave can still be viewed in the older section of Maldon Cemetery in nearby London Road.

ABOVE AND LEFT The abbey pre restoration, both images believed to include John Doyle Field

In 1912 a lease was granted to Captain Frederick Grantham, son of judge Sir William Grantham. Frederick set about the restoration of the abbey and the construction of a range of modern domestic buildings.

This scheme was entrusted to Basil Ionides, who was responsible for a careful and, in the main, sympathetic restoration, while Wykeham Chancellor designed a cottage in the grounds, using as part of its structure the brick remains of an earlier farm building which stood on the line of the west range of the cloister.

Tragedy befell the Grantham family in the Great War. Captain Grantham was killed in action, aged 44, on 9th May 1915 near Richebourg l'Avoué while leading his company of men of the Royal Munster Fusiliers. He was for three months reported wounded and missing, but his body was found by a patrol in August. He was a great traveller in the East, and a student of its sacred books. On one occasion he walked from Siam, via Burma to India, in the company of Buddhist monks, sharing their food and their shelter, and afterwards published a book of practical philosophy, 'the Book of Life and Death'. He was noted for his kindness to his men and his utter fearlessness, and it is said that it was largely due to him that the Munsters reached the German trenches in the engagement that cost him his life. His elder son, Hugo, a second lieutenant in the Essex Regiment, was killed seven weeks later on 28th June, aged 20, while taking part in an attack on a Turkish position at Gallipoli. He had previously been highly commended for "exceptional gallantry and coolness under most trying conditions" and was also mentioned in despatches. A double memorial tablet in marble, complete with regimental badges, to both father and son was erected in All Saints Church Maldon in January 1917.

Captain Frederick Grantham

2nd Lt Hugo Grantham

Following Captain Grantham's death, his widow, ironically a German aristocrat, born Alexandra von Herder of Schloss Salenstein, Thurgau, Lake Constance, continued to lease the abbey for four years. She became a very accomplished, but now all but forgotten, war poet. Perhaps Alexandra should have the last word in relation to their tragic First World War story. In one of her poems she describes herself as one of a "multitude of mothers who, with trembling hands, grope in the darkness, waiting for sons who will never return". She also wrote a number of books on Chinese history and porcelain between 1918 and 1939. She had left the abbey by 1919 and married a Norwegian, Johann Wilhelm Normann Munthe, from Bergen.

After a military education in the cavalry, Munthe emigrated to China in 1887 where he became a cavalry instructor under General Yuan Shikai, and was the first foreigner to become a lieutenant general in the Chinese army. Consequently, Alexandra then lived most of her remaining life in China. Munthe died in 1935. Interestingly, another of Frederick and Alexandra's sons was Sir Alexander Grantham, Governor of Hong Kong from 1947 to 1957.

In 1920 the abbey itself and its immediate surroundings were sold by Sidney Samuel Baker, grandson of Benjamin and Frances Baker, to Jessie Harriette, wife of Richard Edwin Thomas, who together continued to restore the abbey and, in 1930, commissioned the architect Wykeham Chancellor to improve the gardens. Following Jessie Harriette's death, Richard Thomas continued to live at the abbey until 1945.

RIGHT
A painting of
Beeleigh Abbey
mid 19th century
by Robert
Nightingale
1815 - 1895
hangs in the
calefactory

BEELEIGH ABBEY

On 19th and 20th April 1921, 'St Roger His Ring', a musical play by A J Gregory Nicholson, was performed in the grounds of the abbey. It was set in 1289, the year when King Edward I and Queen Eleanor visited the abbey, and was based on the loss and subsequent discovery of the large gold ring which once belonged to Saint Roger of Beeleigh, and which was bequeathed to the abbey church by Alice de Bledlawe in 1311.

1921

To commemorate the 750th anniversary of the abbey, on 28th June 1930, a series of episodes from the history of the abbey was presented in the grounds by the Essex County Drama Society. Tickets for numbered seats for the afternoon performance at 3 o'clock were sold for 5s. and 2s. 6d, and standing room for 1s. 0d. Tickets for numbered seats for the evening performance at 6.30 were sold for 3s. and 1s. 6d, and standing room for 6d. Tea was offered at the abbey for a moderate price.

1921

1930

The abbey
pre-restoration
early 20th century

The abbey
pre-restoration
early 20th century

The abbey
post restoration
c 1925

Secular owners and residents of the abbey

1537 - 1546	Sir John Gates (or Gate) of Garnetts (beheaded 1553 on Tower Hill – a supporter of the Duke of Northumberland and Lady Jane Grey)
1546 - 1548	William Marche of Calais
1548 - 1549	William Marche (son of above)
1549 - 1552	Joan Franke (wife of William Marche)
1552 - 1580	Thomas Franck
1580 - 1627	Richard Franck
1627 - 1633	Sir Leventhorpe Franke
1633 - 1653	Thomas Craythorne
1653 - 1662	Robert Ingram
1662 - 1698	Richard Ingram (son of above)
1698 - 1699	John Bludworth
1699 - 1725	John and Utritia Bludworth
1725 - 1737	John Bludworth (son of above)
1737 - 1740	Sarah Clifton
1740 - 1750	Thomas Snell
1750 - 1776	John Fortescue MB
1776 - 1778	Sir John Duntze of Devonshire (and others)
1778 - 1801	Abraham Shuttleworth and Benjamin Rosewell
1801 - 1860	Frances Baker
1860 - 1920	- Baker
c1890 - 1911	John Doyle Field (tenant resident)
1912 - 1915	Captain F M Grantham (lessee)
1915 - 1919	Alexandra Grantham (widow of above - lessee)
1919 - 1920	Samuel Sidney Baker
1920 - 1943	Jessie Harriette and Richard E Thomas (Richard Thomas sold to William Foyle in 1943 but remained in residence until 1945)
1943 - 1963	William Alfred Westropp Foyle and Christina Foyle
1963 - 1976	Christina Foyle (widow of William above)
1976 - 1994	Christina Foyle (Batty) (daughter of above) and Ronald Batty (her husband)
1994 - 1999	Christina Foyle (Batty – widow of Ronald Batty)
1999 - 2000	Executors of Christina Foyle (Batty)
2000 -	Christopher and Catherine Foyle

Abbey coat of arms.
Six fleur de lys.
Set above main entrance

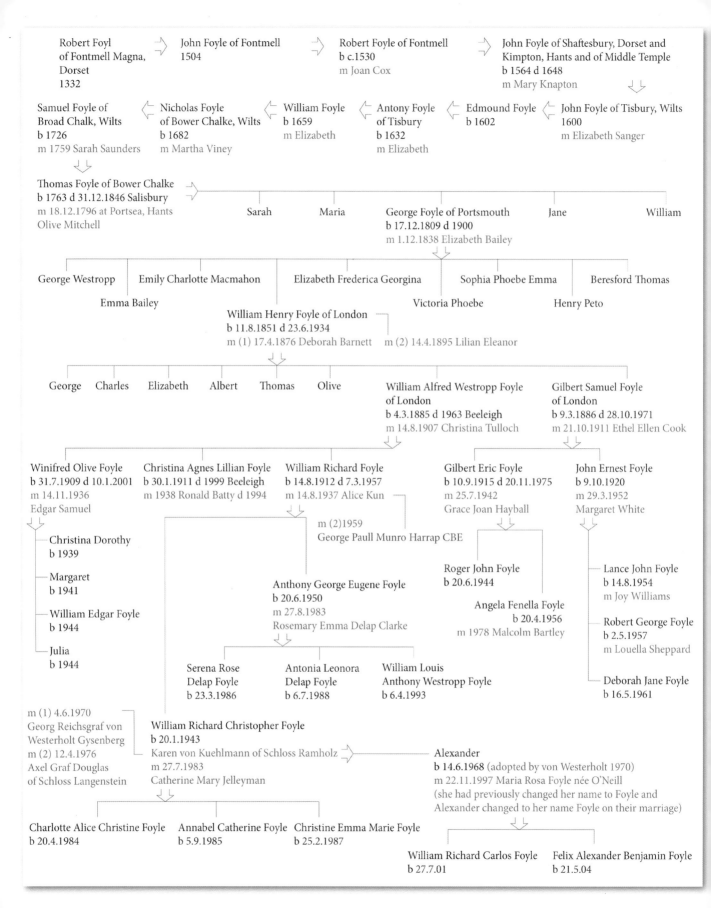

Robert Foyl
of Fontmell Magna,
Dorset
1332

→ John Foyle of Fontmell
1504

→ Robert Foyle of Fontmell
b c.1530
m Joan Cox

→ John Foyle of Shaftesbury, Dorset and
Kimpton, Hants and of Middle Temple
b 1564 d 1648
m Mary Knapton

Samuel Foyle of
Broad Chalk, Wilts
b 1726
m 1759 Sarah Saunders

← Nicholas Foyle
of Bower Chalke, Wilts
b 1682
m Martha Viney

← William Foyle
b 1659
m Elizabeth

← Antony Foyle
of Tisbury
b 1632
m Elizabeth

← Edmound Foyle
b 1602

← John Foyle of Tisbury, Wilts
1600
m Elizabeth Sanger

Thomas Foyle of Bower Chalke
b 1763 d 31.12.1846 Salisbury
m 18.12.1796 at Portsea, Hants
Olive Mitchell

Sarah · Maria · George Foyle of Portsmouth
b 17.12.1809 d 1900
m 1.12.1838 Elizabeth Bailey
· Jane · William

George Westropp · Emily Charlotte Macmahon · Elizabeth Frederica Georgina · Sophia Phoebe Emma · Beresford Thomas

Emma Bailey · Victoria Phoebe · Henry Peto

William Henry Foyle of London
b 11.8.1851 d 23.6.1934
m (1) 17.4.1876 Deborah Barnett   m (2) 14.4.1895 Lilian Eleanor

George · Charles · Elizabeth · Albert · Thomas · Olive · William Alfred Westropp Foyle
of London
b 4.3.1885 d 1963 Beeleigh
m 14.8.1907 Christina Tulloch
· Gilbert Samuel Foyle
of London
b 9.3.1886 d 28.10.1971
m 21.10.1911 Ethel Ellen Cook

Winifred Olive Foyle
b 31.7.1909 d 10.1.2001
m 14.11.1936
Edgar Samuel

Christina Agnes Lillian Foyle
b 30.1.1911 d 1999 Beeleigh
m 1938 Ronald Batty d 1994

William Richard Foyle
b 14.8.1912 d 7.3.1957
m 14.8.1937 Alice Kun

m (2)1959
George Paull Munro Harrap CBE

Gilbert Eric Foyle
b 10.9.1915 d 20.11.1975
m 25.7.1942
Grace Joan Hayball

John Ernest Foyle
b 9.10.1920
m 29.3.1952
Margaret White

Christina Dorothy
b 1939

Margaret
b 1941

William Edgar Foyle
b 1944

Julia
b 1944

Anthony George Eugene Foyle
b 20.6.1950
m 27.8.1983
Rosemary Emma Delap Clarke

Roger John Foyle
b 20.6.1944

Angela Fenella Foyle
b 20.4.1956
m 1978 Malcolm Bartley

Lance John Foyle
b 14.8.1954
m Joy Williams

Robert George Foyle
b 2.5.1957
m Louella Sheppard

Deborah Jane Foyle
b 16.5.1961

Serena Rose
Delap Foyle
b 23.3.1986

Antonia Leonora
Delap Foyle
b 6.7.1988

William Louis
Anthony Westropp Foyle
b 6.4.1993

m (1) 4.6.1970
Georg Reichsgraf von
Westerholt Gysenberg
m (2) 12.4.1976
Axel Graf Douglas
of Schloss Langenstein

William Richard Christopher Foyle
b 20.1.1943
Karen von Kuehlmann of Schloss Ramholz
m 27.7.1983
Catherine Mary Jelleyman

→ Alexander
b 14.6.1968 (adopted by von Westerholt 1970)
m 22.11.1997 Maria Rosa Foyle née O'Neill
(she had previously changed her name to Foyle and
Alexander changed to her name Foyle on their marriage)

Charlotte Alice Christine Foyle
b 20.4.1984

Annabel Catherine Foyle
b 5.9.1985

Christine Emma Marie Foyle
b 25.2.1987

William Richard Carlos Foyle
b 27.7.01

Felix Alexander Benjamin Foyle
b 21.5.04

The Foyle family

The Foyles were a West Country family, the earliest references to them being at Fontmell Magna in Dorset in the early 14th century. In the latter part of the 16th century a branch migrated just across the county border into Wiltshire, to Tisbury and Wardour, where John Foyle, a lawyer, became steward to Lord Arundell of Wardour Castle. John amassed lands and estates in Dorset, Wiltshire and Hampshire. A painting of one of his descendants, the Reverend Edward Foyle of Kimpton, hangs in the calefactory of the abbey.

Most of these Foyles fought for the king in the Civil War. One of them, Oxenbridge Foyle, was arrested and imprisoned for taking part in the Penruddock uprising against Cromwell and, without trial, was shipped across the Atlantic and sold as a slave in the sugar plantations in Barbados, although he later found his way back to England following the restoration of Charles II.

A descendant of one of John Foyle's kinsmen, Thomas Foyle, moved in the late 18th century from Bower Chalke in Wiltshire to Portsmouth. One of his sons, George, moved to London, and in 1843 founded Foyle & Co, a wholesale groceries and dry salting business, which his son William inherited. William had a large family of whom only his eldest, George, took on the business.

William's seventh and eighth sons, William and Gilbert, took exams to enter the Civil Service. They failed them and advertised their used textbooks for sale. The response was such that they bought more for resale, and from these beginnings in 1903, Foyles, which became the world's largest bookshop, was born.

In the 1930s, William Foyle, one of the two co-founders, got to know and love this corner of Essex. He used to sail on the Crouch and Blackwater rivers, with his friend A J A Symons, the author of 'The Quest for Corvo'. One story is that he first caught sight of Beeleigh Abbey from the Chelmer, while another was that he first saw it whilst walking past. In either case, he fell in love with it.

He approached Richard Thomas, by then a widower, and purchased the abbey in 1943. However, William Foyle made an agreement with Richard Thomas that he could continue to live at the abbey as a tenant, until he decided to move, which he did in 1945, which is when William Foyle, together with his wife Christina, began to live at the abbey.

ABOVE
Coats of Arms relating to the Foyle family
c. 1590 to 1640

OPPOSITE
The Foyle family tree

In the document evidencing the sale, Richard Thomas required William Foyle to enter into a covenant that the abbey would never be used for Roman Catholic practices or services. To enforce this covenant, Richard Thomas retained the freehold, with rights of access, of a small plot of land in the grounds which he leased back to William for 99 years.

During the 1940s and 1950s William Foyle gathered a large collection of rare and antiquarian books and manuscripts, ranging from a 10th century Greek manuscript and works from every subsequent century to books published and bound in the 20th century. He housed this magnificent library in the long, first floor room which was in monastic times originally the dorter or dormitory (sleeping quarters) of the canons.

During the eighteen years he lived at Beeleigh Abbey, William Foyle was a generous and hospitable host to those who visited or stayed there. He would delight in showing them the many fine volumes in the library, such as Shakespeare's First, Second, Third and Fourth Folios and the large number of medieval manuscripts, including illuminated books of hours handwritten on vellum. He might have invited you to indulge in his Bassett-Lowke gauge 'O' steam and electric model railway layout in the large attic room, or to a game of croquet or bowls on the lawn after tea, followed by dinner in the evening, accompanied by Châteauneuf du Pape, madeira, brandy, Benedictine, cigars and a game of cards.

He lived life to the full. He loved to play practical jokes on his many visitors and guests. He wore his long mane of white hair swept back down to his shoulders, a three piece suit with gold watch chain and fob watch, and wing collar and cravat fixed with a diamond or pearl tie-pin. He rose at five every morning and would be heard singing in the bath. We grandchildren enjoyed lighting the incense in the chapel censer and pumping the Handel organ while William played it.

In March 1955, William Foyle delighted in welcoming to the abbey the first Premonstratensian Abbot since the dissolution, Father Norbert Backmund, the Abbot of Windberg Abbey in Bavaria. Father Norbert, a great scholar, had written a three volume history of the Premonstratensian Order in Latin, two sets of which are in the abbey library.

William and Christina Foyle in James I bedroom

Christina Foyle

William Foyle, a generous and hospitable host

William Foyle with Father Norbert Backmund,
the Abbot of Windberg Abbey

Following William Foyle's death in 1963, his widow, Christina, continued to live at the abbey until she died in 1976, when it then became the residence of William Foyle's second daughter Christina Batty, better known as Christina Foyle, and her husband Ronald Batty. Christina and Ronald ran Foyles from 1945, Christina continuing after Ronald Batty's death in 1994 until her own death in 1999. She was particularly known for her famous Foyles Literary Luncheons, founded in 1930, and which then ran uninterruptedly several times a year, at the Dorchester or the Grosvenor House. Most of the great figures in literature, politics, the arts, theatre, the media and the military, spoke at or attended these luncheons from 1930 until 2007. They included General de Gaulle, General Sikorski, Emperor Haile Selassie, the Duke of Edinburgh and all the British prime ministers since the Second World War except for Sir Winston Churchill, Tony Blair, Gordon Brown and David Cameron. Margaret Thatcher was given three luncheons – one for each of her three books.

LEFT
Ronald Batty
in the library

BELOW
Beeleigh
Abbey today

Following Christina Foyle's death, as a result of her will, a large part of the most important items of the library had to be sold, but the abbey, most of its contents and part of its library, and the surrounding land, were purchased by one of William Foyle's grandsons, Christopher Foyle, the author of this book, and his wife Catherine.

ABOVE
Christopher and Catherine Foyle

Richard Thomas's grandson, Bob MacGregor, by then 89 years old, was contacted by Christopher Foyle in 2004 and together with his wife and son invited to the abbey on a number of occasions. Christopher and Catherine Foyle purchased the freehold of the plot of land that had been excluded from the sale in 1943 from Bob Macgregor and his relatives. Bob MacGregor's mother was the daughter of Richard Thomas. Bob's father died when he was six, in 1921, and so he went to live with his grandparents at the abbey for many years, which is where he grew up. He recalled that lighting came from portable oil lamps and fixed gas mantles. The gas was town gas from Maldon.

The roof and part of the fabric and structure of the abbey and contents had deteriorated during the preceding thirty years. The Foyles, with the aid of Ed Joslin, their right hand man at the abbey, and with the wisdom and advice of David Andrews of Essex County Council, Paul Drury and a team of specialist builders, craftsmen, joiners, engineers and upholsterers, embarked upon a four year programme of necessary but sensitive restoration and repair of the building and its contents, and the gardens and grounds.

A gratifying consequence of this was the 2007 Maldon District Council Building Conservation Award, followed in 2008 by the RICS East of England Award, and later that year, by the RICS National Award for the best restored and conserved historical building in the whole of the United Kingdom.

HALL HOUSE EXCAVATION

ABBEY BUILDINGS

ARCHAEOLOGY

From 2001 to 2006 systematic archaeological investigations were undertaken in the abbey grounds by the Maldon Archaeological and Historical Group (MAHG), following a promising geophysical survey in 2001 of the main garden lawn and the paddock to the west of the abbey.

The magnificent work over several years by the volunteers of MAHG was supervised by David Andrews and by archaeologists Howard Brooks and Trevor Ennis from the Colchester Archaeological Trust and the Essex County Council Field Archaeology Unit.

Excavations in the paddock field to the west uncovered a group of medieval domestic buildings associated with the service area of the abbey. The earliest identified feature was a hearth made of roof tiles dated to c.1225-1265, apparently associated with a timber building all other traces of which had disappeared. As the excavation proceeded, there emerged the almost complete foundations of a medieval hall house comprising, from south to north, parlour, open hall, cross-passage providing access, and service rooms for provisions. Three hearths were uncovered in the process: one in the parlour associated with a wooden chimney; a central open hearth with tiles laid vertically on edge, smoke from which would have been emitted through the roof; and a third with a brick chimney which superseded the open hearth. There were also rear extensions. The date of the hall house is uncertain, but may well have been constructed in the second half of the 13th century, and it definitely had a long life. The most significant improvements to the house were the remodelling of the parlour end as a cross-wing, and the construction at the end of the 15th century of a large brick chimney at one end of the hall backing on to the cross-passage. The finds indicate that the house went out of use and was pulled down at about the same time that the abbey was dissolved in 1536. To the north of the hall house, evidence indicated a detached kitchen building and to the north of that, a smithy.

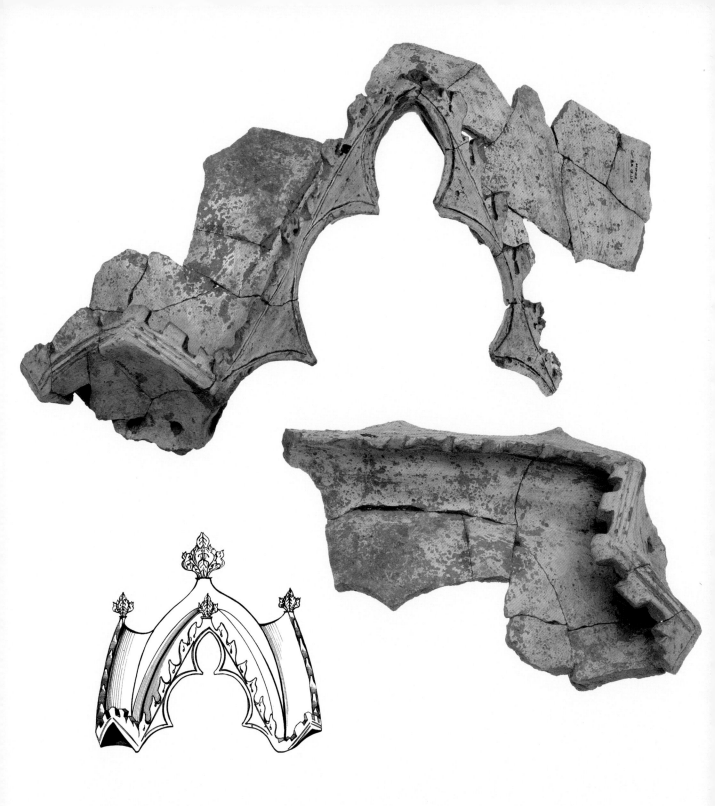

The Beeleigh Louver

Louvers were fitted into the ridge of a roof normally for the emission of smoke from a hearth below but also as ventilators for kitchens. The remains of the louver found at Beeleigh sugggest it to be very decorative and impressive and possibly more so than any others recorded in Essex. An artist's impression of reconstructed Beeleigh louver is shown.

IMAGES NOT TO SCALE

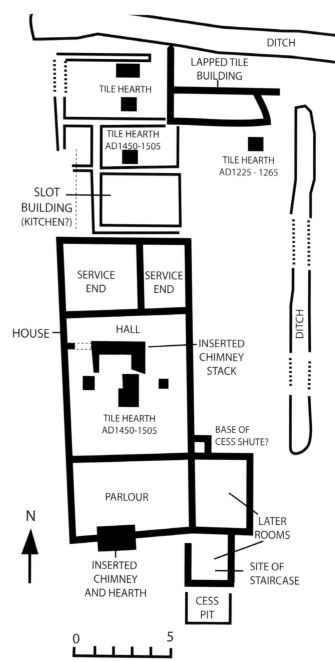

CLOCKWISE

A small oil lamp from Holland

Drawing of the site

View of hall house site looking north 2003. The cess pit is in the foreground

Two very small pots possibly used as vessels for condiments to hold wine and water during the church service

The good quality of the glass found indicates that it must have come from the destruction of the abbey when it was converted into a country house

At work on the site

A pot being excavated

DITCH

LAPPED TILE BUILDING

TILE HEARTH

TILE HEARTH
AD1450-1505

TILE HEARTH
AD1225 - 1265

SLOT BUILDING (KITCHEN?)

DITCH

SERVICE END

SERVICE END

HOUSE

HALL

INSERTED CHIMNEY STACK

TILE HEARTH
AD1450-1505

BASE OF CESS SHUTE?

N

PARLOUR

LATER ROOMS

INSERTED CHIMNEY AND HEARTH

SITE OF STAIRCASE

CESS PIT

0   5

METRES

45

Later excavations in 2004 on the east side of the field revealed a long building with a large hearth with a timber-framed chimney. The size of the building and its proximity to the abbey suggests that it might have been the abbey kitchen, bake house or brew house. Further excavations in 2005 revealed several unexpected features, indicating that the building may have had a first floor, strengthened by the discovery of a perforated brick associated with the malting of barley, leading to the conclusion that ale was brewed on the site.

In the north east corner of the field, excavations revealed a clamp for firing bricks. Unlike a kiln, a clamp was usually a temporary structure made out of the unfired bricks themselves. Clamps had the advantage of being able to fire much larger quantities of bricks than early kilns. The Beeleigh clamp probably produced about 100,000 Tudor type bricks. Research into documentary evidence indicates that this brick clamp predated the dissolution, but this does not, of course, preclude the possibility that its use continued after the dissolution.

Frank Gardiner's impression of (from right to left) hall house, kitchen and smithy
based on archaeological evidence (late 15th century/early 16th century)

Over 200 kilos of pottery were excavated, spanning the late 12th to mid 16th centuries, most being made of locally made red earthenware, some produced in the Colchester area. As well as the usual jugs, cups, bowls and jars, there were a number of more specialised vessels. Imported pottery was also present, mainly German stoneware, but also from Beauvais in France and from the Netherlands, including a tin-glazed maiolica vase of a type sometimes used as altar vases.

Other artefacts included a wide variety of coins and jetons or counters and a number of miscellaneous items such as a seal matrix from Beeleigh Abbey in very good condition.

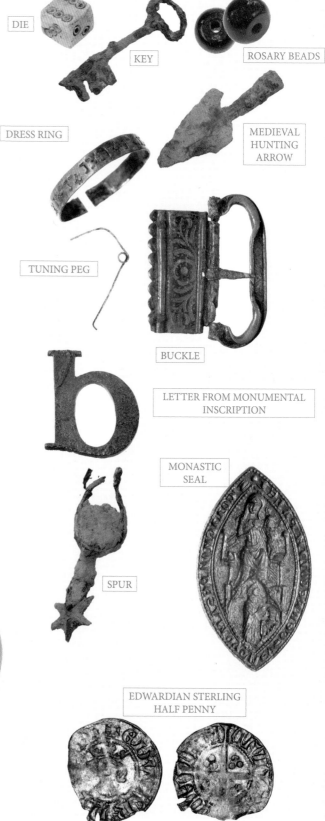

DIE

KEY

ROSARY BEADS

DRESS RING

MEDIEVAL HUNTING ARROW

TUNING PEG

BUCKLE

LETTER FROM MONUMENTAL INSCRIPTION

MONASTIC SEAL

SPUR

EDWARDIAN STERLING HALF PENNY

A SMALL BUNGHOLE JUG APPARENTLY FOR A LEFT-HANDED PERSON

IMAGES NOT TO SCALE

A particularly interesting find was a fragment of a stone carving a little over two inches in height. It consisted of two hands cupped around a heart shaped object still showing traces of pink paint between the fingers and blue paint on the cuffs. It is tempting to surmise that this fragment might have been part of an effigy representing hands holding the casket containing the heart of St Roger of Beeleigh, particularly as it is very similar in appearance to another shrine effigy that survives in Scotland.

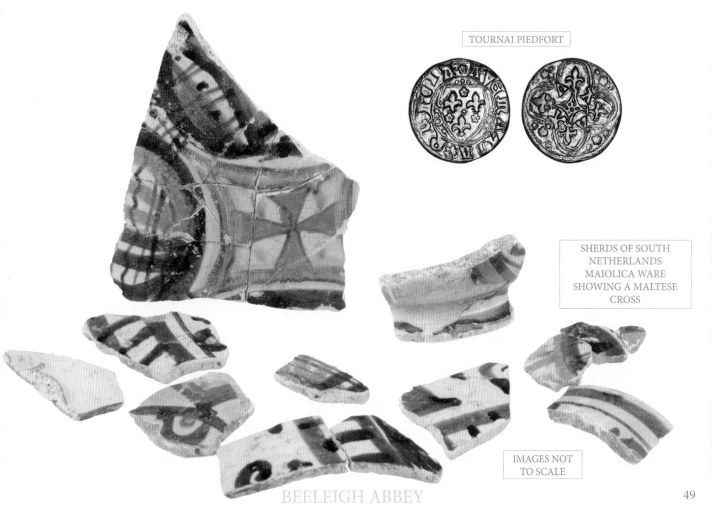

TOURNAI PIEDFORT

SHERDS OF SOUTH NETHERLANDS MAIOLICA WARE SHOWING A MALTESE CROSS

IMAGES NOT TO SCALE

Visitors Today

In recent years, thousands of visitors have enjoyed timetabled openings of the grounds. There have also been pre-booked tours of the house led by local historian, Stephen P Nunn, who has had a life-long interest in the history of the abbey.

In 2006 David Grantham, great nephew of Captain Grantham, together with his family, from New Zealand, were welcomed to the abbey.

In October 2007, the Air League of the United Kingdom, of which Christopher Foyle was then chairman, hosted a banquet at Lincolns Inn in London, on the occasion of the sixtieth anniversary of the United States Air Force. General T Michael Moseley, its chief of staff, interested in English history, had heard about the abbey and expressed a wish to visit it. He and his staff of twelve, together with others including Lord Petre, the Lord Lieutenant of Essex, and Leo McKinstry, historical aviation author, were welcomed to luncheon and given a conducted tour.

EXPLORE
ESSEX
ITS QUICKER BY RAIL
Full information from any L·N·E·R Office or Agency

245   Extremely rare Essex poster of Beeleigh Abbey by Schabelsky

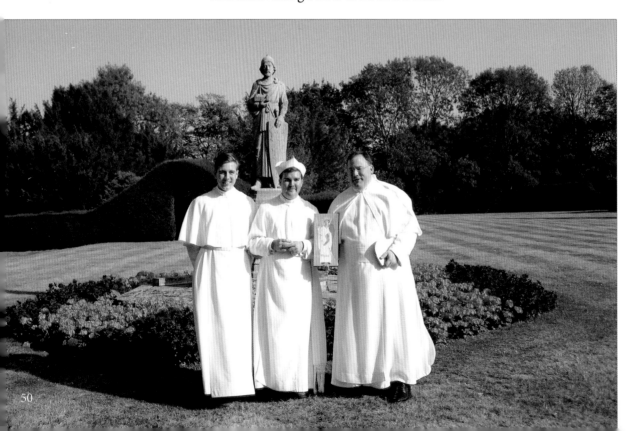

In 2009, Father Hugh Allan, the prior of the newly formed Premonstratensian Priory in Chelmsford, together with two of his canons and a novice, were welcomed to the abbey, and in 2011, from Rome, none other than the abbot general of the Premonstratensian Order, Thomas Handgraetinger. The story of the abbey, it would seem, has turned full circle.

LEFT Father Hugh Allan with one of his canons and a novice in the garden during their visit in 2009. ABOVE A visit to the abbey in 2011. Christopher Foyle with Thomas Handgraetinger, Abbot General of the Premonstratensian Order, on his right and Father Hugh Allan, Prior of Chelmsford, and canons and novice in the library. By permission of Newsquest Essex.

THE ABBEY SITE AND BUILDINGS

Beeleigh Abbey stands about 150 yards from the right bank of the River Chelmer, about three-quarters of a mile west north west of Maldon. It can be reached directly by a footpath from the town of Maldon or by driving west out of Maldon on the old London Road. About half a mile along this road, a by-road to the right eventually leads to the turning to the abbey.

A stretch of wall in Tudor brick along the lane may be all that remains of the precinct boundary, but may post-date the dissolution. The original gatehouse (later called the 'Longhouse') probably stood close to the by-road near the modern gateway.

The central feature of every monastery was the cloister, a square open court surrounded on all four sides by roofed and sometimes vaulted passageways. The canons used these alleys as their general living quarters where they studied and worked and where the novices were instructed.

The church usually stood on the north or less often the south side of the cloister, the choice being governed by the lie of the land or the whereabouts of the water supply. At Beeleigh the church was to the north of the cloister, its site now occupied by gardens and a pond. The area where it stood had been dug over in the 19th century for gravel and any foundations that might have remained were grubbed up, except, possibly, at the west end.

The monastic cloister was flanked on its other three sides by the main domestic buildings of the house. These usually followed a predictable arrangement. The east side was occupied by the chapter house, parlour and warming room with the dorter or dormitory on the first floor above them. The south side was devoted to the frater or the refectory, either on the ground floor or raised on an undercroft. The west side formed the department of the cellarer and had a store room on the ground floor with apartments above it usually used in small houses to house the more important guests. Generally to the east of the main block was a detached group of buildings called the farmery or infirmary where the old and sick resided, often connected to the cloister by a covered passage. The remaining buildings were usually grouped round an outer court entered immediately from the great gatehouse. They included bake and brew houses, barns, stables and a limited amount of accommodation used by those members of the laity whom the abbey had promised to supply with food and lodging.

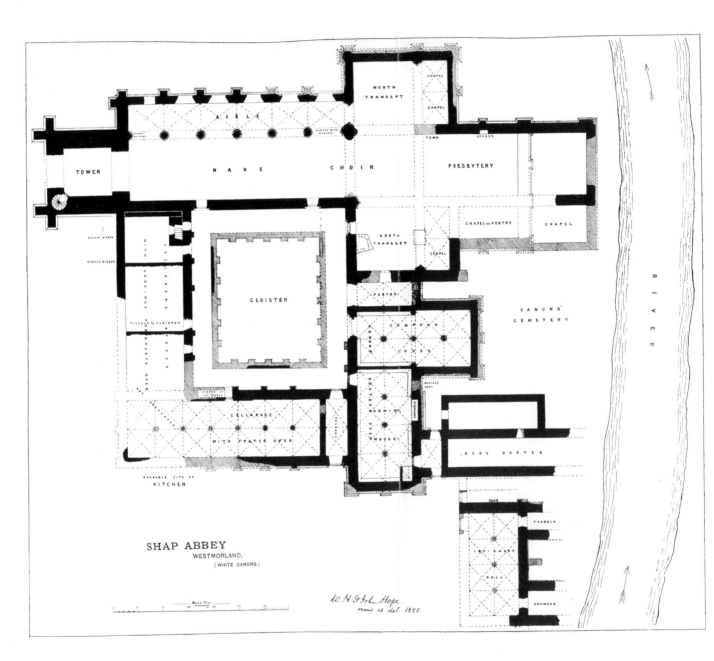

Shap Abbey, Westmorland is also of the Premonstratensian Order.
The layout is almost identical to Beeleigh Abbey.

In the case of Beeleigh Abbey, the dissolution of 1536 and possible additional later destruction resulted in the demolition of the church, the west and south ranges flanking the cloister court together with most of the outbuildings including the infirmary and stables, but we do not know exactly when each of these buildings was actually demolished. Thus the existing remains of the abbey consist of the major part of the range flanking the cloister court on the east side, and a small portion of the range of buildings on the south side, to which have been added a 17th century timber-framed building extending further south incorporating some remains of the original monastic building. This timber-framed building has been tree-ring dated to 1624, when the abbey belonged to the Franck family.

The walls of the abbey, where ancient, are mainly of roughly coursed blocks of dark brown conglomerate or ferricrete, a type of iron pan formed in deposits of gravel. It occurs locally, evidence for quarrying being found in the paddock excavations. The dressings for windows and doorways are being mainly of Reigate stone, a soft type of Greensand that carves readily but weathers badly.

Key to plan opposite

1. Dorter Undercroft or Warming House (ground) and Dormitory or 'Great Chamber' (above)
2. Children's Chamber (above)
3. Dining Parlour or Refectory/Frater (above)
4. Possible site of the Outer Court or Yard (ground)
5. Cloister (ground)
6. Chapter House (ground)
7. Chamber (ground) and 'The White Chamber' (above)
8. Stairway space and chest store (ground and above)
9. Servant's Chambers (ground and above)
10. 'Another Chamber' (ground) and 'The Green Chamber' (above)
11. Bakehouse (ground)
12. Brewhouse (ground)
13. Church - Canons' Choir (ground)
14. Church - Our Lady Chapel (ground)
15. Church - Jesus Chapel (ground)
16. Church - St Katherine's Chapel (ground)
17. Church - Rood Chapel in North Aisle (ground)
18. Vestry (ground)
19. Kitchen (ground)
20. Buttery (ground)
21. Infirmary or 'The Fermory Chamber' (ground)

Existing remains shown *xxxxxxx*.
Possible site of the Heart Shrine of Saint Roger shown ✚

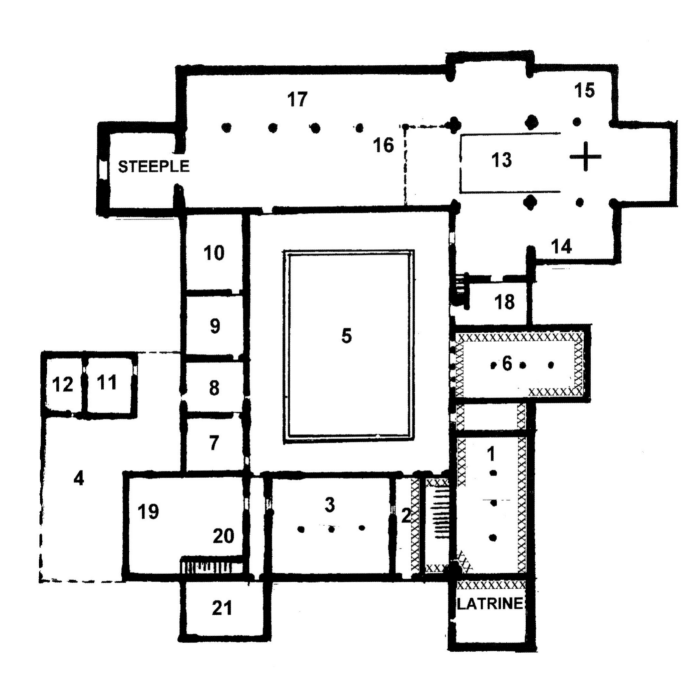

STEEPLE

17 16 15 13 14

10
9
8
7

12 11

4

19
20
21

5

6

18

1
2
3

LATRINE

Conjectural plan of Beeleigh Abbey
c 1536 (after Petchey in MAG 1985)

The Chapter House

The chapter house was where the business affairs of the abbey were conducted by the abbot, duties were allocated, punishments issued and a 'chapter' of the Rule (of St Augustine) was read on a daily basis.

The chapter house is datable to the early 13th century. It is a rectangular building measuring 40ft by 19ft and divided into two aisles by a row of three octagonal columns down the middle. The vaulted roof has eight quadripartite bays with moulded transverse, diagonal and wall ribs of Reigate stone and vaulting webs of chalk. The easternmost bay and the third bay from the east have bosses at the intersections carved with foliage.

The west wall of the chapter house contains a pair of delightful doorways in Reigate stone with Purbeck marble columns, flanked by windows with early tracery. Of the other chapter house windows, there are only two original survivals, one each in the north and south walls. They are lancets, single lights with pointed arches, although that in the north wall has been given a cinquefoiled head. The other windows are all 15th century replacements of two lights with cinquefoiled arches below flat heads. In the western bay of the south wall of the chapter house is a modern doorway opening into the adjoining passage or parlour.

In the chapter house is a cross made from oak stated to have been cut from the "Monks' Ladder" in the monastery at St Albans in use c.1270 with a figure of Christ said to be the work of Benvenuto Cellini during his exile in Naples c.1529.

By the 19th century the state of Beeleigh Abbey had deteriorated to such an extent that the chapter house was being used to house cattle and pigs.

In the north west corner stands the chamber organ, acquired between 1920 and 1922 by Richard Thomas from Sacombe Church in Hertfordshire. Whilst at times attributed to Snetzler and also to Dr Morse of Barnet, it was more likely built in 1747 by Thomas Parker. It was known to have originally been in the Foundling Hospital in London, where Handel often played, and it was known as Handel's organ. Indeed, it is said that he composed his Largo on this organ.

Handel opened the organ in person on 1st May 1750 with a performance of the Messiah. All the tickets, and they cost half a guinea a piece, were sold out at Batson's Coffee House and White's Chocolate House (later White's Club) days before. Many distinguished persons, who had neglected to purchase tickets in advance, drove up to the doors believing that they would obtain seats without difficulty. Some of these were subscribers to the hospital funds – could they be turned away? The result was inevitable. They were sold seats that had already been sold to someone else and, when the real owners of the seats arrived, they had perforce to go home again.

This displeased Handel, who had never yet issued tickets for a concert that he had not honoured sooner or later. He announced a second performance for 15th May at which every ticket sold for the first concert but as yet unhonoured should take precedence. It was an act of grace, which brought further funds to the hospital and enabled Handel to keep faith with the public, for the second performance of the Messiah in the hospital chapel was as successful as the first.

By 1999 Handel's organ was in poor condition. In 2001, a three year overhaul and refurbishment of both the works and the case was commissioned, and beautifully executed.

Handel's organ,
refurbished

The Parlour

The original monastic plan would have included two parlours, one used for conversation between the canons, and one called the outer parlour where conversation was allowed between the canons and their lay relatives and friends. The outer parlour was usually on the west side of the cloister. The parlour in Beeleigh Abbey was therefore the one used for conversation between the canons.

The parlour or passage adjoining the chapter house on the south is a narrow apartment 21ft by 10ft with a plain barrel vault. In the west wall is a high pointed archway of the 13th century forming the former entrance from the cloister but now leading to the kitchen wing, built in around 1912. At the east end of the room is a pointed doorway of the 13th century with the remains of a former label or hood-mould. This had been blocked, but in the late 20th century it was replaced with an arched stained glass window, commissioned by Christina Foyle and executed by the British master glass painter John Hayward in 1978, with panels depicting the various phases of the abbey's history and ownership.

This window shows St Roger at the high altar with his heart above. This demi-figure is balanced by the seated figure of St Norbert, the founder of the Premonstratensian Order, and above them, the arms of Beeleigh. Between them is the abbey seal and their canopies are topped by the patron saints, SS Mary and Nicholas. The founder of the abbey, Robert Mantell, is seated on the right, holding a small version of the abbey, and the most important line of benefactors and patrons, the Bourchiers, are represented on the left, with their arms beneath. The Bourchier tomb, indicated as a typical canopied monument, is placed under St Roger.

The dissolution is suggested by the busy passage at the bottom left, with the royal arms stained on to white glass with the HR monogram in the centre. The abbey falling into a state of disrepair, with cattle grazing in the chapter house, is shown in the bottom corner. The whole thing then passes to Sir John Gates, shown with sword and standard breaking across the abbey plan.

The rest of the window is concerned with the later years. In the cloisters are two groups of figures, one planting trees, the other engaged in rebuilding, both under the aegis of Grantham, shown as a letter G. Above, the fireplace in the calefactory becomes a hearth with a fire, suggesting the abbey as a house for William A Foyle rather than a museum. Underneath, the abbey as it now is, with small figures set in a cross section, reading and working in the library.

In the lower corner, a visitors' book contains the names of some of the writers, artists etc who have visited the abbey. Christina Foyle and her husband Ronald Batty are shown as two seated figures with their names linked in a hatchment above.

The side walls of the parlour have remains of the original painted decoration including a band of conventional foliage ornament between two red lines, and some painted lines also in red in imitation of masonry. In the south wall is an opening of more recent date leading to the undercroft.

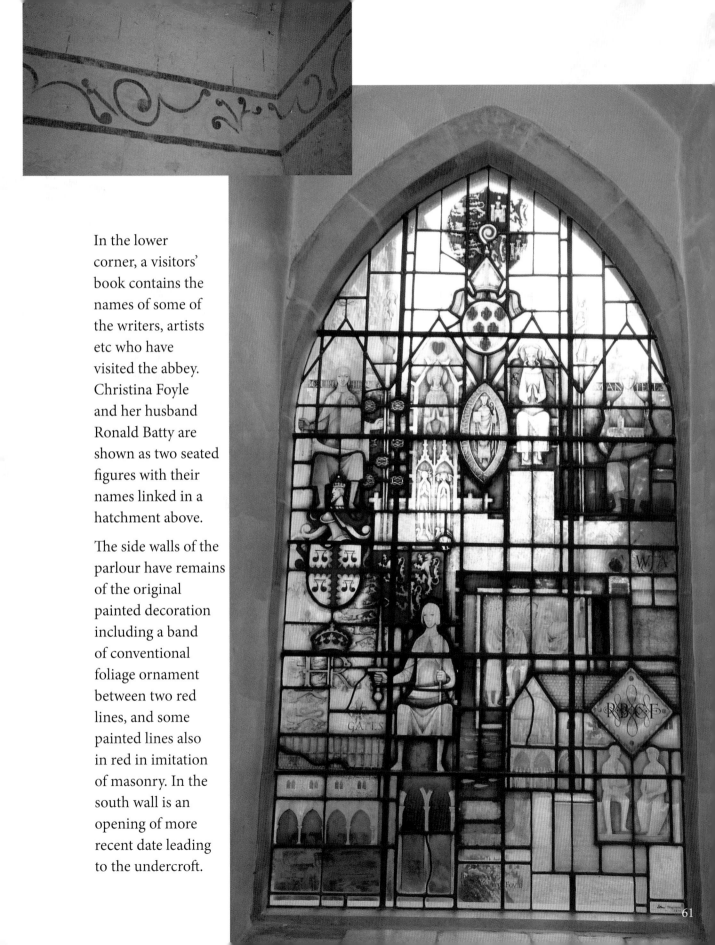

The Dorter Undercroft or Calefactory

It was customary in the Benedictine and Augustinian orders to use the sub-vault under the dorter as a warming room or calefactory. In the houses of the Premonstratensian canons, the dorter undercrofts of Shap, Alnwick and Dale were provided with fireplaces and therefore must have been used as the warming houses of those abbeys. We can assume that the sub-vault at Beeleigh formed the monastic warming house or common room, the only room in the abbey where the rule permitted a fire for the warmth and comfort of the abbot and the canons.

ABOVE Alexander, son of Christopher Foyle and Karen von Kuehlmann of Schloss Ramholz

RIGHT Bronze Lion and Bronze Antelope, both by Loet Vanderveen b.1921, in the calefactory.
The Black Panther by Florencio Cuiran, in stone, 1939, in the calefactory

BELOW Charlotte, Annabel and Christine Foyle, the three daughters of Christopher and Catherine, a painting on the main staircase

63

Robert Devereux, 2nd Earl of Essex of that name. Favourite of Elizabeth I. Beheaded 25th February 1601. After Marcus Gheeraedts the Younger. In the calefactory.

The dorter undercroft is a long apartment, 42ft by 21ft, extending southwards from the parlour. It is four bays long with a row of three circular Purbeck marble columns down the middle and has a stone vault with chamfered diagonal and transverse ribs of Reigate stone in a very perfect state of preservation. On the northernmost column are a number of 15th century graffiti, two being names, apparently Lyghtwod and Lychfeld. The vault webs, as in the chapter house, are of chalk blocks but there are no wall ribs. Against the walls the vaulting springs from moulded corbels with varied terminations including a knotted spiral and stems enriched with a wreath of flowers and a crown-like ornament of six fleurs de lis. In each of the three northern bays of the east wall is a 15th century window of three cinquefoiled lights with a transom and vertical tracery in a pointed head with a moulded label. The northernmost window has been almost completely restored. The southernmost bay of this wall previously had a window corresponding to those in the other bays and of which the outline is still visible externally. It has been subsequently blocked and in the blocking is a 17th century doorway with an oak frame, a pointed head and an oak door of ridged battens with chamfered fillets. It still has its quaint iron knee-shaped knocker. Between the windows are two-stage buttresses of which the upper stage has been rebuilt in early 16th century brick.

The back of the fireplace in the west wall is built out into the south range of the cloister, into the space once occupied by the stairs to the first floor dormitory. The removal of these stairs, and the formation of a room over them, probably took place around 1513, the date obtained from the roof over this surviving end of the south range. The stone fireplace is impressive and betrays classical influence in its frieze. It has a wide segmental arch with spandrels panelled with quatrefoils and enriched with plain shields, lions' faces and flowers. Above the arch are the carved and embattled cornice and the frieze carved with six angels holding musical instruments that have been identified as the rebec, gitterne, shawm, psaltery, portative organ and drums. Flanking the head of the fireplace are small vertical shafts finished with embattled capitals.

In the southernmost bay of the west wall is an original 13th century doorway with chamfered jambs, pointed arch and segmental rear-arch. The south wall of this room contains two 13th century doorways. The eastern one of the two has an oak door studded with nails and divided into panels by moulded ribs. It is probably 15th century. Traces of the original decoration remain on the north wall where there is a band of conventional foliage similar to that in the parlour.

LEFT
A young lady described as Countess of Essex: after Jacopo Robusti, called II Tintoretto, in the 'Exhibition of the Royal House of Tudor', New Gallery, London 1890

RIGHT
A portrait of the Reverend Edward Foyle, Rector of Kimpton in Hampshire (d1784), by Arthur Devis

Above the original doorway in the west wall is a painting of a cock with an extravagant enrichment to the tail feathers. Clapham suggested that this is late 16th century, but some believe that it could be a rebus (or visual pun) for Abbot Cokke who was poisoned by a canon of the abbey, John Ultyng, in the early 15th century.

On the north wall hangs a portrait of the Reverend Edward Foyle, Rector of Kimpton in Hampshire, and on the west wall a portrait of a Countess of Essex attributed to Tintoretto.

Stained glass in the Calefactory

Set in the windows on the east side are seven panels of ancient glass originally in the abbey, removed for a time to Maldon Hall, but then restored to the abbey in the early 20th century. All the windows of the abbey, as well as those of the church, as of the principal rooms, were filled prior to the dissolution in 1536 with stained and painted glass. None of this has survived today with the exception of these seven small panels. The huge quantity of coloured window glass found in the paddock excavations indicates that the painted windows were removed for reuse soon after the dissolution, and the plain glass discarded.

Of these panels, six are single figure subjects, each representing a saint standing under a canopy against a coloured background, blue or ruby. The figures and their canopies are entirely in grisaille, heightened with yellow stain and the canopies are all alike in design. The leaf-diapering of the coloured backgrounds are, also, all of the same pattern. The other panel, which represents the Blessed Trinity, is in grisaille with yellow staining in parts without colour.

The saints represented by the single-figure subjects are Our Lady with a pot of lilies by her side and an open book in her left hand; the Archangel Gabriel, leaning, bearing a sceptre and with a scroll on which is the angelic salutation; another of the Archangel Gabriel; St John the Evangelist, in his left hand a book, on which stands an eagle, his symbol; St John the Baptist with a book on which is the Holy Lamb; a sainted bishop on a pedestal, labelled Augustin, various contradictions on this piece of glass make it almost certain that the bishop in this picture is not St Augustine, but is certainly a sainted bishop. It has suggested that this substituted figure may be intended to represent St Roger of Beeleigh.

The picture of the Blessed Trinity on the seventh piece of glass has been remounted to match the other six. In its original state, however, it was a roundel, within a circular border, made up of a running stalk and leaf design, containing a representation of the Trinity – God the Father enthroned, holding, before him, a cross bearing the hanging figure of our Lord, with the Holy Ghost in guise of a dove, above Our Lord's head.

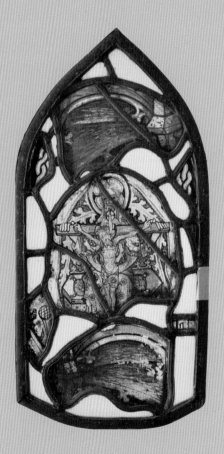

The design and general style of these old glass pictures indicate that they would probably be from the last quarter of the 14th century. However, examination of the brown enamel work, especially the shading, combined with the fact that the glass is cut from crown glass of a size which was not made until the 15th century, means that they were probably painted in the first half of the 15th century, probably by an old craftsman working in the style of his youth.

Also set in one of the windows is a rectangular panel, featuring nine heads, in three rows of three, mostly English, in white glass with silver stain, including three of the late 14th/15th century in the middle row and the centre top, whilst bottom right is early 16th century Netherlandish.

In addition to the items described above, a large collection exists of many different dates, consistent in its sympathetic evocation of the period, history and fabric of the abbey, from authentic medieval panels, through heraldry of many dates, to the Gothic Revival glass of the 19th century, and more recent panels on chivalric or historical themes.

The development of enamel painted glass, from the 16th century, is represented by a high quality Swiss or South German heraldic panel of the 16th or early 17th century and by two roundels of the 17th and 18th centuries. Such circular, or oval, panels were very popular in domestic settings from the late Middle Ages, being placed on focal points in clear glass windows. A large and delightful group of decorative panels is painted on thin greenish glass with birds or flowers, probably made in Holland in the 17th and 18th centuries.

The two most interesting of the Gothic revival panels are the strange procession by moonlight and the panel of the royal arms of England. The first is typical of the early 19th century Romantic interest in the medieval past. The second is an accomplished copy of part of the original glazing for Henry VIII's hall in Hampton Court Palace. This may be by Thomas Willement, a specialist in heraldic art.

The Dorter or Dormitory (now the library)

The dorter was where the canons originally slept. It was customary to divide the dorter into separate cubicles with wainscot partitions for each canon. Windows with brick surrounds inserted into the walls of this range at first floor reveal the positions of the individual cells they were designed to light. In each cell was an oak bedstead, with mattress, sheets, wool coverlet and pillow. At the head of the bed was a shelf for clothes. At the foot was a wooden stool and beside it a rush mat. As midnight drew near, the abbot or prior passed through the dormitory, flashing his lantern into each cell. Shortly after, the sub-sacrists who had watched all night before the high altar rang the bell for matins and all rose from their beds, said the creed and gloria and two by two, preceded by a novice with a rush light, entered the ante church and then through the crossing at the transepts, went to their places in the choir.

However, the dissolution inventory of 1536 describes this room as the Great Chamber indicating that the canons no longer slept here but would have had individual accommodation. It had two beds and curtains and a fireplace, and "old cloths and tapestries" on its walls, so presumably served as accommodation for the earls of Essex and the Bourchier family, the abbey's patrons. The inventory describes a number of chambers in the west range, demolished after the dissolution, which served as more comfortable lodgings for up to six canons and three or four servants.

William Shakespeare, a portrait, English School after the Chandos portrait. In the library

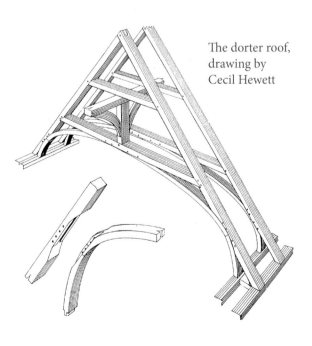

The dorter roof, drawing by Cecil Hewett

Sir Walter Scott 1813
by Thomas Phillips RA.
In the library

Charles Dickens as a young man 1840
by Daniel Maclise.
In the library

The dorter is a long apartment 46ft by 21ft lit by a range of five early 16th century windows in the east wall. These windows are mainly of brick and are each of two pointed lights under a square head with a moulded label. Similar windows in the west wall were blocked up in 1912. In this west wall is a stone doorway with a four-centred head and a rebate on the inside. It may possibly be connected with the former day-stair to the dorter, but is more probably a post-reformation reuse of old material. The north end of the dorter is now separated from the rooms over the chapter house by a timber-framed partition, probably of the 17th century and containing a square-headed doorway of that period. The opposite or south end of the room also has a timber-framed partition, probably of the 16th century and inserted after the dissolution. The framing shows evidence of the former existence of three doorways, but only the western most of these is now in use. On the face of the original studs are peg holes for some fixture, now gone. The partition has a moulded oak cornice of late 15th or early 16th century date and above it is a close screen, not in situ and consisting of thirteen and a half panels divided by oak buttresses with moulded heads, offsets and bases. The screen is finished with a moulded cornice. It is unlikely that the framing and screen had a use in the monastic dorter and so were probably introduced after the dissolution. It is possible that one of the early lay owners turned the dorter, when the monastic buildings were reduced to their present limits, into his great hall and inserted a pre-existing screen, brought from elsewhere, perhaps from the destroyed frater, at its south end.

ABOVE William Foyle in the library. RIGHT Example of medieval illuminated manuscript, typical of those in the library. LEFT Medieval illuminated manuscript in the centre of the table.

The oak roof of the dorter has been tree-ring dated to 1511-1539, a date range being given because the timbers lack sapwood. It must have been built towards the beginning of that period as it pre-dates the dissolution, and is yet more evidence of the intensive building activity that was being carried out at the beginning of the 16th century. It is of crown-post type with curved braces and ashlar pieces below forming four-centred arches and giving the roof a wagon form, a type of construction very rare in Essex. Originally, the timbers were covered with lath and plaster, but they are now exposed.

Behind the screen at the south end is a narrow lobby formed out of the southern most bay of the former dorter. In the south wall at the east end is a 13th century doorway with chamfered jambs and pointed arch, which was probably the entrance into the rere-dorter where the canons' toilets were located. Further west in the same wall is a mid 16th century doorway with a three-centred head opening into the timber-framed wing. In the west wall is a plaster doorway with a four-centred head of the 16th century. Adjoining this doorway is a mid 16th century staircase leading up to the third storey over the southern frater range.

The room above the chapter house probably formed part of the dorter from which it is still only separated by the 17th century partition. Today, it is divided by more partitions into various rooms and the outer walls are modern, except for that on the south side and the adjoining portion of the east wall. One of the coloured illustrations of the abbey in the 'Historical Account of Beeleigh Abbey' by George Draper, published in 1818, shows the upper level above the chapter house still standing, but illustrations of the mid and later 19th century show it to have disappeared, to be rebuilt by Captain Grantham in 1912 under the supervision of Basil Ionides. As a result, the windows at first floor are all modern, though often of reused material. They replicate the ground floor pattern of lancets and two-light windows with cinquefoiled arches beneath flat heads.

The dorter or dormitory of a monastic house was originally a large apartment generally in direct communication with the church by means of a staircase known as the night stairs, and used by the religious at the night offices. This staircase commonly descended into the transept, often by a broad flight of steps such as still remains at Hexham Priory. A second staircase called the day stairs descended from the dorter to the cloister. The exact position of the day stairs can now be determined, but not that of the night stairs.

The position of the rere-dorter cannot be definitely fixed but it probably stood to the south of the dorter range and connected with it by the short two-storied corridor that still remains. If this assumption is correct, there still survives of the rere-dorter a short length of the north wall adjoining the corridor and having a broken face at the east end showing that it formerly continued further in that direction.

Since 1920 the dorter has served as the library. William Foyle installed his magnificent collection of antiquarian books and medieval manuscripts here, and many of them remain here today. High on the north wall hangs an early wind instrument, the serpent. On the east wall hangs an uncharacteristically severe portrait of William Foyle by Dugdale, and another of Christopher Foyle by Zsuzsi Roboz. High on the south medieval screen, are portraits of Christopher Foyle, his wife Catherine and their daughter Charlotte, also by Roboz.

William Foyle by Dugdale

The Frater

The frater range flanked the south side of the cloister, but with the exception of the easternmost bay, it was destroyed some time after the dissolution. This bay contains on the ground floor the usual passage at the end of the frater, communicating between the cloister and the court to the south, and on the first and second floors two quite large rooms now used as bedrooms. Forming the entrance to the passage, and now the main doorway to the house, there is a 13th century doorway with chamfered jambs and a two-centred arch. To the east of it is a two-light window with an oak frame, probably of the 18th century. Above the doorway is a modern corbel copied from one that was originally in All Saints church, Maldon, and having a shield with the arms attributed to the abbey.

Dendrochronological analysis of the timbers of the surviving frater roof indicates a date of 1513/14, i.e. late pre-dissolution, indicating that these rooms were built in the early 16th century as part of an upgrading to make the abbey more comfortable and domestic. Perhaps the chamber on the first floor comprised the later abbot's lodgings.

The Lodgings

OPPOSITE ABOVE Pentice Chamber partly covered by 13th century tiles

BELOW King James I bedroom previously known as the Pentice Chamber

Today, there are a number of bedrooms containing Jacobean tester or four poster beds. Five of these beds were acquired by William Foyle in August 1943 from Hall Place, Bexley, Kent, previously in the ownership of May Countess of Limerick.

One particularly superb example is in the attic bedroom above the first-floor chamber in the frater, in what is now called the James I Room, previously known as the Pentice Chamber. It was known as the Pentice Chamber until the 1912 restoration by Captain Grantham, and until then was partly covered by 13th century tiles, hundreds of them, lying loose on the undulating floor. A Mr Parry who, at one time, was about to buy the abbey from the Bakers, took three of them to his home. When Richard Thomas bought the abbey, all these tiles had disappeared but, to his great delight, Mr Parry gave him his own three specimens. These have now been set in the chapter house floor.

The headboard of the bed is inlaid with a carving of King James I, with the eye of God looking down on him. This bed was in the abbey before William Foyle's ownership and is reported to have come to Beeleigh from Malmesbury in Wiltshire, where it was previously situated in Charlton Park, the seat of the Earls of Suffolk and Berkshire, though how, when and why it came to Beeleigh is not known. It was said that James I slept in this bed when visiting Charlton on progress in 1620. The bed has been dated to c.1620 with a framework of the time of Henry VII. The James I Room is one of the rooms reputed to be haunted – by the ghost of Sir John Gates of Garnetts.

ABOVE
The boudoir

RIGHT
Another bedroom
nearby, known as the
Henry Bardon Room,
has its walls painted in
trompe l'oeil. Christina
Foyle commissioned the
designer and artist Henry
Bardon to carry this out
in 1972, and these were
restored in 2004 by the
present owners.

Some strange goings on

Shortly after Christina Foyle's death, her manager was closing doors in the abbey prior to going home in the early evening. As he walked through the calefactory, away from the door he had just closed, leading to the stairs going up to the dorter, there was a loud bang and the door shook hard "as though someone was trying to rattle it from the other side". Frightened, he did not then go to find out what had caused it. The next morning he went to investigate and found nothing that could have caused the noise.

Not long afterwards, a security firm was hired to stay and protect the abbey as nobody was in residence. One night, the security guard on duty was in a room leading to a passage with the door to the rest of the abbey closed and locked, watching television. He heard breathing and then sneezing on the other side of the door. He unlocked and opened the door, but there was nobody there.

During restoration work, there were a number of unexplained incidents in the James I Room, supposedly the most haunted room in the abbey. After the work began, the estate manager found that the four poster bed had an indentation in the mattress and covers, as if somebody had been lying on the bed. When it was re-made, the indentation would then appear on the other side of the bed. This continued to happen for a number of weeks. There was never any sign of indentations on the pillows.

While painting the stair well from the calefactory to the dorter, the painter felt what he described as somebody patting him on the shoulder. He looked around, expecting to find someone had crept up on him, but there was nobody there.

Whilst a four poster bed was being put back together, all the components were laid out in the right place and checked, to make sure that everything was present and correct. When it got to the last piece to be put in, a bolt, it had disappeared. Three days later, the bolt was found in the middle of the floor, on a landing at the other end of the abbey.

When laying the oak floors, the joiner went into a small cupboard under a staircase to obtain some materials. He heard heavy breathing and smelt what he described as bad breath.

THE GARDENS

The gardens evolved over many years under John Doyle Field, Captain Grantham, Richard and Harriette Thomas, William Foyle, and now Christopher and Catherine Foyle. From 1976, the gardens suffered a steady deterioration from their previous high point. By 1999, the great borders had lost most of their flowers, shrubs and plants. The many paths had lost their edges and were muddy and weed infested.

A programme of improvement commenced in 2000, under John Angel. He brought the gardens back from years of neglect, reclaiming the gravel paths, weeding and replanting the original mixed borders. In 2006, Chris Cork became head gardener. His first tasks were to maintain existing parts of the garden and to develop new ones. The combined ideas of the Foyles and Chris Cork have resulted in the development of new areas and a large number of new plantings in recent years.

The gardens are surrounded by mature trees on most of the boundaries that shelter them from strong winds. But that and the location on a north-east slope down to a river makes for something of a frost pocket. The soil is mainly clay and of neutral PH. Work has been done in recent years to improve soil structure and drainage by adding organic matter, manure, compost and grit.

Attempts are made to work with nature where one can by restricting the use of pesticides to glasshouses, by using organic fertilisers where possible, and making compost from leaves, grass clippings and soft prunings. Birds are fed and nest boxes put up. There are areas of the garden where the grass is left long - in the wild flower meadow and the orchard, for example.

On the main lawn to the east of the abbey stands the statue of Sir Robert de Mantell, founder patron of the abbey. It was commissioned by William Foyle from the sculptor Frederick Brook Hitch, and erected in 1945.

TOUR OF BEELEIGH ABBEY GARDENS

As you go through the gardens, please be aware of the changes in levels, uneven steps and open water.

Entering from the car park, to the right you will see the front driveway of the house.

Front driveway

The border in front of the cottage measures 3m x 10m and is backed by an oak pergola. It was designed by using classic cottage garden plants but in a more formal manner than the main cottage garden because of its position. It is also designed to showcase the rest of the garden. To the left is the canal planted up with marsh marigolds and water lilies. Across the driveway are ten iceberg climbing roses covering 30m of the Tudor brick wall. These are under planted with hydrangeas and spring flowering bulbs.

Pond and woodland area

Retrace your steps to where the gravel path splits and go straight on through a wooded area. Trees include oak, ash, laurel and yew. Several log piles have been made for the benefit of wild life and invertebrates. This area looks particularly good in spring with snow drops, aconites, narcissus and bluebells. Continue down the path for beautiful views of the tidal river Chelmer. If you turn right where the path splits and walk along the side of the abbey's chapter house, you will see the pond on your left which is planted up with white water lilies, arum lilies and flag irises. Around the pond there are many dogwoods (Cornus sibirica, flaviramea, mid winter fire) and the ornamental bramble (Rubus thibetanus). Then follow the path round to the left and you come to the newly planted marquee border.

Marquee border

Mixed shrubs are under planted with seasonal bulbs, including narcissus and tulips in spring, and lilies in the summer. Shrubs such as azaleas, hydrangeas and cornus give interest for many months of the year. If you continue round to the right you will come to the spring border.

Spring border

This is planted up with camellias, azaleas and rhododendrons, and under planted with a large number of scented pheasant-eye narcissus and purple flowered tulips.

Scented border

Opposite the spring border and backed by the Tudor wall, many of the shrubs and flowers chosen here are scented; for example, yellow flowered honeysuckle, mahonias, jasmine, nicotianas and sweet peas. Continue along and you enter the kitchen garden.

Kitchen garden

Two borders 37m long; the left backed by the Tudor brick wall, and the right by espalier apples and pears. Half way along a pear arch leads to the wild flower meadow. The kitchen garden includes a cut flower area growing twelve varieties of sweet peas, gladioli, dahlias and summer annuals. There are also raspberry, strawberry and asparagus beds, and many vegetables including red and white onions, shallots, garlic, beans (runner, dwarf and broad), four varieties of lettuce, early and main crop potatoes, sweet corn, courgettes, marrow, carrots, parsnips, celeriac, beetroot, and herbs. Walk through the pear archway to the wild flower meadow.

RIVER CHELMER

yew hed walk

river walk

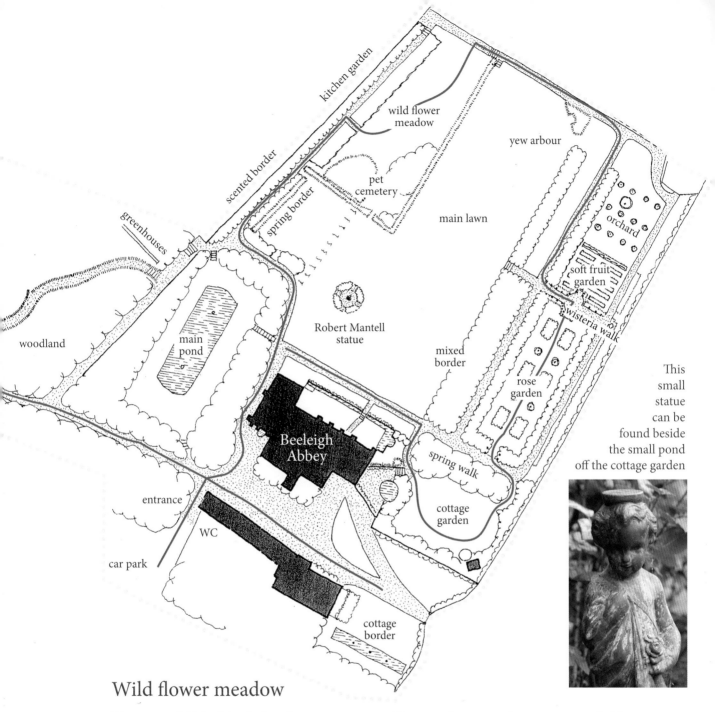

This
small
statue
can be
found beside
the small pond
off the cottage garden

Wild flower meadow

The area of 532m² includes the pet cemetery. The meadow contains many cornfield species, for example field poppy, ox-eye daisy, corn cockle, cornflower, corn marigold, field scabious, musk mallow and red and white campion. The meadow is mowed annually in September once the seed has dropped, all the debris is raked off and the ground lightly cultivated. Follow the snaking mowed path to the steps; at the top of the steps you will find yourself at the back of the main lawn with a great view of the abbey.

Continue along and then take a right turn to bring you to a large mulberry tree and the start of the two large mixed borders.

Mixed borders

These run either side of the gravel paths and are 78m long divided half way on one side by the wisteria walkway and on the other by the path and steps leading to the main lawn.

Trees, shrubs, roses, perennials, grasses, bulbs and annuals provide something of interest during most of the seasons. Planting in these big borders is often in large groups: roses in threes, and perennials in fives, sevens or nines of one species. The use of buxus and large perennials like acanthus and cynara helps to give real structure.

Half way down the path, on the left is the wisteria walkway.

Wisteria walkway

This divides the soft fruit garden from the rose garden. The wooden framework is made of oak and is 18m long x 2m wide. There are four varieties of wisteria which include W. rosea, violacea, floribunda, longissima alba and sinensis alba. This provides different flower colour, form and prolongs flowering time. This is under planted with lavender hidcote and for spring colour white narcissus, tulips and alliums.

Soft fruit garden

This is positioned to the left of the wisteria walkway and is backed on the other three sides by fan-trained plums. The fruit includes gooseberries, blackcurrants, white currants, raspberries, rhubarb, and six varieties of strawberries. Behind the soft fruit garden is the orchard.

Orchard

This includes apple, pear, cherry, plum and medlar trees. The orchard is divided from the soft fruit garden by a line of fan-trained apple trees.

Rose garden

Turn right out of wisteria walkway into the rose garden. There are 33 different varieties of the English old rose and English leander hybrids, a total of 425 plants. There are six island beds 3m x 5m, and on the left hand side there is a bed 43m x 2m which runs the whole length. At the far end, two further beds 4m x 4m are separated by a rose archway. Three wigwam structures made of oak post and rope supports add height to the long border. There are a further four wigwams on the bank opposite.

On leaving the rose garden through the archway you pass a small stumpery.

Stumpery

Made up of large timber, plants include ferns and white foxgloves. Opposite is a shady area planted with hostas, ferns and lily of the valley. Walk a bit further to enter the cottage garden.

Cottage garden

Contrasting with the more formal areas, the cottage garden has no straight lines; all the borders are curved. On the edge of a small circular patio, an old potting shed helps to create an 'olde worlde' feel. The planting is a lot more random to give a feeling of self seeding. It includes repeat flowering old roses, scented shrubs (Philadelphus), perennials such as delphiniums, lupins, and foxgloves, and annuals such as cosmos, antirrhinums and nicotianas.

On leaving the cottage garden turn left and this brings you to the front of the abbey.

Bedding displays

The beds at the front of the abbey and around the statue of Robert Mantell are planted out with seasonal bedding. The summer displays include geraniums, petunias, begonias and antirrhinums. Cleomes are used to give height. Winter flowers include pansies and violas which are under planted with tulips for spring display.

Trees

Notable trees include a tulip tree (Liriodendrom tulipifera), an Indian bean tree (Catalpa Bignonioides), a large mulberry tree, and six large magnolias.

Books by the Granthams

Frederick William Grantham

Book of Life and Death (A revised and enlarged edition of Life, Ideals and Death published in March 1913.) 1921 John Lane the Bodley Head

Alexandra Grantham

Dissolution 1536-7 Suffered by Brother Ambrose, of Beeleigh Abbey, Temp. Henry VIII. Compiled from Ancient Records. London: The Eastern Press

Hills of Blue – A Picture Roll of Chinese History - From Far Beginnings to the Death of Ch'ien Lung, AD 1799. 1927 London: Methuen.

The Little Mermaid 1906

A Manchu Monarch – An Interpretation of Chi Ch'ing 1934 London: George Allen & Unwin.

Mater Dolorosa (poetry) 1915 London: William Heinemann

Montezuma; or, The Blessed Virgin of the Roses a miracle drama in three acts, on the Spanish Conquest. 1911 Women's Press

Pencil Speakings from Peking. 1918 London: George Allen & Unwin

Porcelain Pagodas and Palaces of Jade – Musings of an Old Collector Dedicated to General and Mrs William Crozier. New York: E P Dutton

River Roundels. (poetry) 1905 & 1943 Oxford: Joseph Vincent

Rococo – The Life and Times of Prince Henry of Prussia 1726-1802 1914, 1921 & 1939 New York & London: D Appleton-Century

The Wisdom of Akhnaton. 1918 London: John Lane, the Bodley Head

Bibliography

Anderson, L T 1955: Saint Norbert of Xanten – A Second St Paul, Dublin: M H.Gill

Baskerville, G 1949: English Monks and the Suppression of the Monasteries, London: Jonathan Cape

Bond, J 1993: The Premonstratensian Order : a preliminary survey of its growth and distribution in medieval Europe, in In Search of Cult: archaeological investigations in honour of Philip Rahtz, ed. M. Carver, Woodbridge: Boydell and Brewer

Clark, A 1907: Buried Treasure at Beeleigh Abbey, The Essex Review, 16

Colvin, H M 1951: The White Canons in England, Oxford

Draper, G 1818: Beeleigh Abbey, Essex, London: Draper, Colnaghi & Hookham

Eden, F S pre February 1916: The White Canons of Beeleigh, Catholic Fireside

Fitch, E A c. 1890: The Illustrated Guide to Beeleigh Abbey. Being an extract from "Maldon and the River Blackwater", Maldon: Gowers.

Fowler, R C Clapham, A W & others 1922: Beeleigh Abbey – Essex London: R E Thomas & Co

Fowles, H J 1936: Beeleigh Abbey, Essex, East Anglian Magazine No.9

Foyle, W A 1962: Beeleigh Abbey - A Short History, London: W & G Foyle Ltd

Foyle, W R Christopher 1999: The Family of George Foyle of Portsmouth 1809-1900, Luton: Privately printed

Foyle, W R Christopher 1997: John Foyle of Shaftesbury and Kimpton 1564 to 1648 - His Family and Descendants, Luton: Privately printed

Galpin, F W 1921: St Roger His Ring. A Play of Beeleigh Abbey in the 13th century. April 1921, The Essex Review, No.118

Graham, R 1939: An Essay on English Monasteries, London: G. Bell & Sons

Grantham, A E 1917: Dissolution 1536-7 Suffered by Brother Ambrose, of Beeleigh Abbey, Temp. Henry VIII. Compiled from Ancient Records. London: The Eastern Press

Gribbin, J 2000: The Premonstratensian Order in Late Medieval England, Woodbridge: Boydell & Brewer

Hughes, L 1909: Beeleigh Abbey. An Appendix to A Guide to the Church of All Saints, Maldon. Maldon: Gowers

Hugo, C. 1734-36: Sacri et Canonici Ordinis Praemonstratensis Annales, 2 vols, Nancy (vol. II, cols. 127-128 for the community at Beeleigh)

Hutchinson, R 2006: The Last Days of Henry VIII, London: Phoenix

Ives, E 2011: Lady Jane Grey – a Tudor Mystery, Oxford: Wiley-Blackwell

Kirkfleet, C J 1943: The White Canons of St Norbert. West De Pere, Wisconsin: St Norbert Abbey

Linton, I 1984: The Book of Maldon, Buckingham: Barracuda Books

Newman, V 2004 Two 'Funeral Wreaths of Broken Song': A mother's poetry of war and grief, University of Essex

Nunn, S P 2009: Maldon, Heybridge and the Great War (1914-1918), Maldon: Maldon Archaeological and Historical Group

Nunn, S P 2001: St Roger of Beeleigh, Maldon: Archaeological and Historical Group

Parry, G 1955: Unpublished notes on Beeleigh Abbey, Overstrand, Norfolk

Petchey, W J 2003: The Abbey before the Reformation, Maldon Website (www.itsaboutmaldon.co.uk/beeleigh-abbey/before_reformation.shtml)

Punchard, D ed 2007: Below Ground at Beeleigh, Maldon: Maldon Archaeological & Historical Group

Rowles, H J c.1923: Beeleigh Abbey – Essex

Spurrell, F 1864: Notes on the Present State of Beeleigh Abbey. Near Maldon, Essex. Colchester: Edward Benham

Tweed, H R B 1916 Some Ruined Shrines of Essex Beeleigh Abbey, Westminster Cathedral Chronicle, vol. 190 No. 2.

Whitfield, J L 1922: St Roger of Beeleigh, Brentwood Diocesan Magazine, no. 9

Wiseman, J F T 1888: Essex Lays and Legends. Ye Legende of Beeleigh Abbey, Chelmsford: Taylor & Robbins

Wright, T 1834: The Picturesque Beauties of Great Britain – Essex, George Virtue

And two large scrap books entitled "Beeleigh Abbey and its Treasures", containing a copious collection of material including photographs, drawings, excerpts from various books and journals, post cards, records of items purchased, newspaper articles, personal anecdotes, collected and assembled by the late William Foyle and Ronald Batty.

Acknowledgments

The section on 'Estate and Income' is contributed by the historians and researchers Dr Christopher Thornton and John Crellin, St Roger of Beeleigh is based on the book by the historian Stephen Nunn, the section on 'The Gardens' is mainly contributed to by Chris Cork, the section on 'Strange Goings On' by Ed Joslin, and I am particularly indebted to Dr David Andrews, Stephen Nunn, Paul Drury and Dr Christopher Thornton for their reading the manuscript and for their many invaluable comments, suggestions and corrections.

The restoration and conservation of Beeleigh Abbey and its gardens, and the production of this book, could not have taken place without the help of many.

Particular gratitude goes to Silas Krendel and the late Clive Eckert, the late Christina Foyle's executors, for enabling us to purchase Beeleigh Abbey and its estate; Dr David Andrews, archaeologist and historic buildings advisor of Essex County Council for his generous advice, help and wisdom over many years regarding the archaeology, history and restoration of the abbey and his helpful comments regarding this guide; Stephen Nunn, historian, for his terrific and knowledgeable enthusiasm regarding the abbey and much generous help and advice for this book; Philip Tolhurst our lawyer for his invaluable assistance and advice regarding the purchase of the house and land and the freehold of the Thomas 99 year lease garden land and many other ongoing matters regarding the estate and for his efficient execution of all matters; Dr Bill Petchey for his historical knowledge and information in the short time available before his untimely death in 2001; Paul Drury, archaeologist and historic buildings adviser, for his enormous help in deciphering the history of the structure and fabric of the abbey; Ed Joslin, estate and project manager, for the coordination and management of all the restoration works and ongoing management of the abbey; Brenda Joslin for extraordinarily multi-faceted activities from running the shop, accounts and reports to painting benches, and recording of contents; Paul Joslin for painting, signage and IT; Anthea Freeman, housekeeper and secretary, for more multi-faceted activities from cleaning to organising the catering and archiving documents; Chris Cork, head gardener, for his labours and vision having brought the gardens to the enormously improved state they are now in; John and Judy Lea for their significant contribution to the organisation of Garden Open Days, liaising with the local authority and the design and production of publicity material; Chris Voisey for the design and layout of this book; Paul Jelleyman, Gordon Freeman, for the photography of the interior and exterior of the abbey and gardens and Paul Joslin, Brenda Joslin, Chris Cork, Rob Cork, John Lea, Judy Lea and Chris Voisey for the photography of the gardens; the late 'Nobby' Clark, of the Maldon Archaeological and Historical Group (MAHG), until his untimely death site director of the Beeleigh excavation; Derek Punchard, Chairman of the MAHG; Howard Brooks and Trevor Ennis for their professional oversight of the archaeological excavations; Pat Ryan for analysing brick work and historical research; Dr Christopher Thornton and John Crellin for their research into historical archives resulting in their contribution to this book; Pyer Carter for his dedicated work on the trees and hedges; Ian Tyers, then of Sheffield University, for the painstaking and highly professional and invaluably informative dendrochronology; Tobit Curteis and his team for the uncovering of further medieval wall painting and conservation; Dr Tim Ayers and Michael Archer for their study, analysis and report on the stained glass; Brian Morton for his expertise and skill in masterminding the repair of the damaged chapter house wall; Peter Wood and Michael Young, and Howell and Bellion, for the three year restoration of the works and case respectively of the Handel chamber organ; Bakers of Danbury for the structural repair of the chapter house wall; Cater Roofing and Chris Starns for the removal, repair and partial replacement of the entire abbey roof and associated works; Gerald Barrett for the sympathetic design of the new metal grille surrounds of the calefactory Purbeck marble column bases; Purcell, Miller Tritton for designing and managing the gutting and internal rebuilding of the 1912 domestic wing; Frederick J French for the demolition and rebuilding of the interior of the 1912 domestic wing; Johnny Clarke for the expert and painstaking laying of reclaimed limestone slabs throughout the whole ground floor of the abbey; P D Lawrence for replacing the entire hot water and central heating system; Bob Surridge and Graham West for the outstanding joinery construction and restoration of oak floors, wall panelling, beds and furniture; Peter Searles for painting and paint restoration; Pat Green, master bricklayer, and Keith Ruffell for the repair of the abbey buttresses and the repair and building of garden walls and lining all the garden paths with brick; Ian Kidman for cataloguing the antiquarian library; the late Victor Chinnery for evaluating the ancient oak furniture; and to the large number of magnificent volunteers, too many to mention, for their years of work during the seasons of archaeological excavations and for helping in numerous ways during Garden Open Days.

Case Studies in the Develc

Agricultural Change
in Nigeria

Kathleen M. Baker

Lecturer in Geography
School of Oriental and African Studies
University of London

John Murray

Case Studies in the Developing World

General Editors   Robert W. Bradnock and Robin Holmes

Agricultural Change in South Asia   Robert W. Bradnock

Urbanisation in India   Robert W. Bradnock

Population and Development in Peru   Clifford T. Smith

Transport and Development in Tropical Africa   Brian Hoyle

Oil and Development in the Gulf   Keith McLachlan and Anne McLachlan

Agricultural Change in Nigeria   Kathleen M. Baker

Tourism and Development in Africa   W. P. Gamble

Case Studies in the Developed World

General Editors   Hilary Winchester and David Pickard

Agricultural Change: France and the EEC   Hilary Winchester and Brian Ilbery

Industrial Change: New England and Appalachia   Michael Bradshaw

Shops and Offices: Locational Change in Britain and the EEC   Michael Bateman

Population Change: The American South   Robert Estall

First published 1989
by John Murray (Publishers) Ltd
50 Albemarle Street
London W1X 4BD

Phototypeset by Pioneer, Perthshire
Printed and bound in Great Britain by
Butler & Tanner Ltd, Frome and London

British Library Cataloguing in Publication Data

Baker, Kathleen
   Agricultural change in Nigeria. —(Case
   studies in the developing world).
   1. Nigeria. Agricultural industries
   I. Title   II. Series
   338. 1'09669

ISBN 0-7195-4497-1

Contents

Acknowledgements

The sources for data used in this book are as follows: G. Andrae, B. Beckman and Zed Books (Fig. 26); R. H. Bates and University of California Press (Table 1); J. Bivins and Dept of Rural Development, Federal Ministry of Agriculture, Lafia ADP (Figures 27–8, Tables 7–10); BP (Fig. 9); R. W. Bradnock (Fig. 11); P. Collier and ILO (Table 2); Cost Recovery Study Team, PRC, cited by O. Areola, A. Faniran and O. Arintola (Table 6); J. Derrick and *African Business* (Table 4); *Economist* Intelligence Unit (Tables 3 and 5); FAO (Figures 2–4, 29); *Financial Times* (Table 3); A. Folayan and Vantage Press (Fig. 5); T. Forrest, J. Heyer, P. Roberts, G. Williams (Table 5); R. J. Harrison Church and Longman (Fig. 30); W. T. W. Morgan and Longman (Figures 12 and 13); *Nigerian News Letter* and *Nigerian Petroleum News* (Table 3); D. W. Norman and Westview Press (Figures 17 and 21); R. K. Udo and E. J. Usoro (Fig. 29). Every effort has been made to contact copyright holders. We will be pleased to rectify any omissions in future printings.

Copyright photographs are reproduced courtesy of: Sarah Errington/Hutchison Library (p. 32 left); Paul Harrison/Panos Pictures (p. 27); Hutchison Library (pp. 2 top and bottom right, 36, 38, 42, 43); Anna Tully/Hutchison Library (pp. 51, 52).

Examination questions are reproduced courtesy of: University of Cambridge Local Examinations Syndicate, Joint Matriculation Board, University of London School Examinations Board, Oxford and Cambridge Schools Examination Board, University of Oxford Delegacy of Local Examinations.

Many people have helped me in the preparation of this book. I would like to thank Robert Bradnock, Dick Hodder, Kathryn Bell, Murray Last, Sue Martin, Paul Richards, Deborah Florsham, Cathy Keable-Elliot, members of the Geography department at SOAS, in particular Debby Potts, and above all my parents, my husband and children. Thanks also to Sue Harrop for drawing the maps and diagrams and to Catherine Lawrence for additional assistance with cartographic work.

K.M.B.

Introduction

Producing enough food in the developing world is one of the greatest needs of today. In recent years, parts of West Africa have suffered needlessly from drought and famine as the environmental resources necessary for food production do exist within the region. Nigeria, West Africa's largest and richest nation, has considerable potential for food production and yet has not been able to help her neighbours to any great extent when food supplies have been scarce. At independence in 1960, Nigeria was nearly self-sufficient in basic foodstuffs and her economy depended on a thriving agricultural export industry. However, over the past two decades, patterns of agricultural production have changed and in spite of massive investment to develop agriculture in the country, Nigeria is not now always able to feed herself.

This book examines the different types of farming in the major ecological regions of Nigeria and shows how, in spite of agriculture's relatively small contribution to GDP today, most Nigerians still depend directly on the land and have not been freed from it by the economic growth that followed the discovery of oil. Many of the problems facing Nigerian agriculture today are the product of errors in decision-making in the political arena rather than at the farm level.

Although overall agricultural output has not grown, some developments have been taking place in agriculture. The case studies of large irrigation schemes in the north, of integrated agricultural development in the middle belt and of the efforts to increase oil palm production in the south bear witness to this. They also suggest that the farmer is probably one of the least to blame for Nigeria's declining agricultural performance.

1
Nigerian agriculture, a struggling sector

Nigeria is justly called the giant of West Africa. It is by far the most densely populated country and Nigerians account for about half of West Africa's population. Nigeria has many more natural resources than most of its neighbours. It has been particularly fortunate in having vast oil reserves. However, apart from its oil, Nigeria is also known among West African nations for the economic chaos and political instability that has plagued it over the past two decades.

Until the early 1970s, agriculture dominated Nigeria's economy but since then oil has held the principal position. Political decisions taken since independence have relegated agriculture to a secondary economic position. As a result agriculture has suffered, and, increasingly, has occupied a back seat in economic terms. Stagnation had set in by the late 1960s and

was even more apparent during the 1970s, the heyday of oil. Agriculture was sadly neglected and allowed to decline at a time when the opportunities for its development and expansion were greater than ever before. This chapter examines some of the changes that have taken place in agriculture.

Agriculture in Nigeria, a brief outline

In spatial terms, farming patterns in Nigeria correspond fairly well to the nation's three main ecological zones (Figure 1): the north (approximately 10° or 10½°N to the northern border), the middle belt (approximately 8°N to 10½°N) and the south (approximately south of 8°N). The boundaries of the three major farming regions are far from precise and one region grades gently into the next.

Figure 1   Nigeria's states and ecological zones

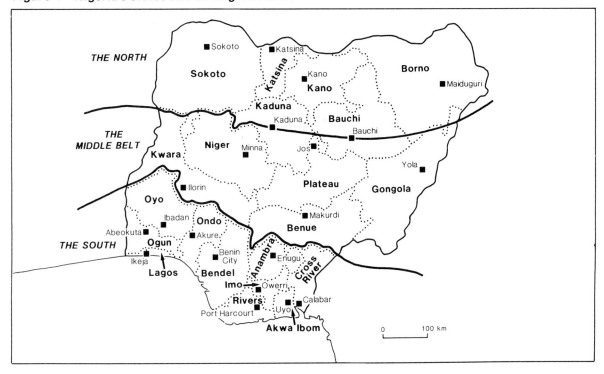

Landscape near Bama (N.E. Nigeria) in the wet season. Compare the sparse vegetation with the forests of the south

Plateau landscape on Jos

The savannas of the north and the middle belt

In the arid north, thin grasses, thorn scrub and dust dominate the landscape. Rainfall ranges from 500–800 mm a year and most of it is confined to the period from June to September. The chief food crops are millet, sorghum, soya beans, cowpeas, some maize and, in the riverine areas, rice. For a long time, cotton and groundnuts have been exported as cash crops but domestic consumption of these has increased and now little is exported. Pastoralism is very important throughout the north and farmers constantly move their herds of Zebu cattle, sheep, goats and donkeys in search of food.

These dry savanna lands gradually give way on their southern side to the more moist Guinea savannas of the middle belt. Here annual rainfall is higher (around 1000–1500 mm), more prolonged and more reliable. Grasses are taller and the bush is more dense. Food crops are more numerous than further north and include sorghum, maize, groundnuts, rice where there is sufficient water, and root crops such as cassava and yams. Groundnuts and cotton were once important cash crops but here, too, domestic consumption has increased and exports have fallen. Pastoralism diminishes in importance in the middle belt as the dense vegetation harbours the tsetse fly. This insect is a vector for sleeping sickness in humans and animals.

The forests of the south

Moving southwards, the atmosphere becomes more sticky and humid as rainfall increases and the vegetation cover is very dense. The rain forest which once covered the south has been largely replaced with secondary forest. Root crops combined with maize, rice and groundnuts are the traditional staple foods, but, as everywhere in West Africa, the diet is supplemented by as wide a range of vegetables as will grow in the area. Tree crops provide most of the

agricultural revenue for the south. Cocoa dominates in the west, rubber in the central southern region and the oil palm—although it is found throughout the south—dominates cash cropping in the south-east. Pastoralism as practised in the north is difficult because of the tsetse fly, but in spite of this most families do keep a few animals, particularly goats, sheep, chickens and breeds of cattle resistant to tsetse. The economic value of these is relatively low. Traditionally, their main use has been to ward off evil spirits from the household.

Nigeria's rainforest, a diminishing resource

2

Nigerian farmers divide their holdings into crops for subsistence and crops for cash. This division has always existed, and even before Europeans came on the scene farmers marketed some of their produce. However, producing crops for a specific market really developed during the early part of the European era, even before Nigeria was truly a colony.

How Europeans influenced farming in Nigeria

From the time of the exploration of the West African coast by the Portuguese in the 15th century, the region was important in the trade in gold, ivory, gum arabic and, from the 16th century onwards, slaves. The British formally abolished slavery in 1807, though it took several years for this move to gain international recognition. It was far from popular at first for slavery had been the main source of revenue from West Africa and, once it was lost, Europeans had to find an alternative reason for maintaining a toehold in the region. The answer was found in West Africa's agricultural products, which were valuable as raw materials for Britain's fast developing industrial revolution.

Palm oil was one of the first West African crops for which there was a demand in Britain. By the 1830s, Britain was importing 10,000 tonnes of palm oil a year and using it for the manufacture of candles, margarine, cooking oil, machine oil and soap. By the 1880s, West Africa was exporting as much rubber as it could to the British market as the recent discovery of the vulcanisation process had greatly stimulated demand. Next came cocoa. This was only introduced to Nigeria and Ghana in the 1880s but was quickly adopted by smallholders. Since then cocoa has grown to be Nigeria's largest agricultural export. Groundnuts and cotton became to the north what these tree crops had become to the south and the export of agricultural products became the foundation of Nigeria's economy. Farmers were more than willing to produce crops for export, so the commercialisation of agriculture occurred early, rapidly and easily in Nigeria.

Measuring change in the agricultural sector

The agricultural patterns developed over almost two centuries have changed considerably in recent years but it is difficult to trace these changes precisely. Statistical data on Nigeria are plentiful but can be misleading. They are at best approximate. Not only are the data-collection methods grossly inaccurate, but many national data are based on uncoordinated and unmonitored samples from different parts of the country. In addition, different methods of analysing the same data can produce very different results. For example, the Central Bank of Nigeria's index of agricultural production for 1982 was 85.5 (1974–76 = base 100). In contrast, the index of production figure from the United Nations Food and Agriculture Organisation (the FAO) for the same year, using the same base, was 130. Not only are the data different but so are the conclusions that can be drawn from them. The question thus remains: what is correct?

As yet, no government in Nigeria, neither military nor civilian, has succeeded in conducting an acceptable census and it is for this reason that the majority of statistics are at best 'guesstimates'. The last acceptable population census was held in 1963. The 1973 census was abandoned. The data were tampered with as a result of the struggle between the major ethnic groups, the Hausa of the north, the Yoruba of the west and the Ibo of the south east, each trying to assert their relative strength in terms of numbers. According to the World Bank, Nigeria's population in 1986 was 116.2 million but, like most other statistics, this too is only an estimate. All statistics from Nigeria have to be treated with caution.

Evidence of decline — what the indicators say

Despite the difficulty with Nigerian statistics, most do indicate a decline in agricultural performance.

The growth rate of agriculture
Agriculture grew at an average rate of 7.8 per cent between 1970 and 1974, the early years of the oil era. As oil became increasingly important in the economy, agriculture grew more slowly. By 1976, growth in agriculture had slowed to about one per cent. Awareness of the need to stimulate the agricultural sector (see Chapter 2) resulted in a slight recovery. Between 1977 and 1979 agriculture is believed to have had a growth rate of around 4.2 per cent. Nevertheless, it was still lagging behind the rest of the economy, where growth was estimated to be around 5.5 per cent. However, government interest in agriculture was short-lived and, as the focus returned to oil, growth in agriculture again diminished. From 1981 to 1985, estimates suggest that growth in agriculture was less than one per cent. According to Hunt and D'Silva (1984), per capita food production in 1981 was probably some 18 per cent below the 1967–70 levels.

The contribution of agriculture to GDP

Until the Nigerian civil war of 1967–70, agriculture dominated Nigeria's economy, contributing some 53 per cent to GDP in 1965. By 1984, its percentage share had almost halved and, as Figure 2 shows, the pattern of Nigeria's economic structure has changed dramatically during the era of independence. However, while agriculture's percentage share of GDP between 1965 and 1984 diminished, the absolute value of agriculture's contribution to GDP increased from $2221 million to $19,832 million. This suggests that although there was a relative decline in agriculture, it may not necessarily have been absolute. However, it is difficult to say whether the rise was due to a real increase in the value of agricultural products or whether inflation in the agricultural sector was so high that it masked the stagnation that many believed was occurring. Studies conducted in rural Nigeria reveal an average annual inflation rate of 30 per cent in the agricultural sector for 1970–80. This is far higher than the average annual rate of inflation for the nation as a whole, which was 18.2 per cent for 1970–78.

Export statistics

Prior to the oil boom, Nigeria's chief exports were cocoa, which was produced mainly by the Yoruba in the south west; palm oil and palm kernels, which were produced mainly by the Ibo in the south east; rubber from other southerners, mainly in Bendel State; and timber from the southern forests. Cotton, groundnuts and groundnut oil, the chief cash crops of the north, tended to be monopolised by the Hausa of the northern States. Over the past 15 years, this long established pattern of commercial agriculture has changed completely and many major exports have declined (Figure 3). Cocoa remains the largest earner of export revenue, followed by palm kernels and products, though in all cases there has been a decline. Exports of rubber and oil palm products have fallen. Palm oil exports have now ceased entirely. Cotton exports have declined to virtually nothing, and no longer figure in the export statistics. Nigeria actually imports cotton and groundnuts now.

Why has there been this fall in exports? There are several reasons. Low prices fixed by or for commodity marketing boards have contributed to low morale in farming since the 1960s. (For a more detailed discussion of the marketing boards see Chapter 2.) Shortly after independence the government began to finance the expansion of its industrial sector on the surpluses from agriculture. The marketing boards creamed off these surpluses in the form of high export and other taxes and paid farmers relatively little for their crops. Table 1 shows the level of some of this taxation. Although this occurred some 20 years ago, the impact is still being felt, particularly in the south.

Figure 3   Trends in some of Nigeria's major exports

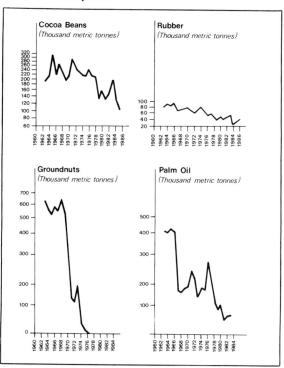

Figure 2   The level and composition of GDP in 1965 and 1984

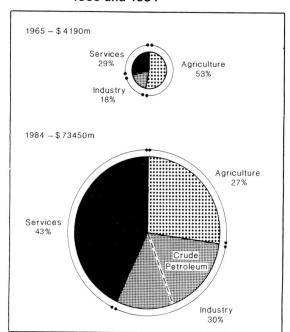

Table 1   Prices paid to the producer for export crops as a percentage of the international price

	Cotton	Cocoa	Groundnuts	Palm oil	Palm kernels
1950–51	16	63	44	61	64
1960–61	25	62	54	63	47
1970–71	36	50	37	49	52
1975–76	—	72	83	(no exports)	150

The relatively high prices in 1975–76 were part of a policy to stimulate the production of export crops.

So disillusioned were southern tree crop farmers that replanting of cocoa trees virtually ceased in the 1960s. In consequence, thousands of cocoa trees are now well past their best bearing years. Disease has weakened them further and yields are low. Efforts in 1973 to restructure the marketing boards and raise producer prices came too late to reverse the trend in production and it will be many years before newly planted trees are yielding fully.

Producers of oil palm have been similarly affected but, unlike cocoa which has little use in Nigeria, some oil palm products can be used domestically. Palm oil exports have fallen to nothing but at the same time exports of palm kernels have continued. The decline in the export of palm oil does not mean that yields are at an all time low but rather that domestic consumption has increased. Having said this, it must be mentioned that production of both palm oil and rubber fell after the Nigerian civil war of 1967–70, owing to neglect of trees and machinery for processing the raw materials.

Drought struck the north between 1972 and 1974 and again in the early 1980s, ruining cotton and groundnut crops, and while higher prices ought to have acted as a stimulus for field crops, exports of these fell too. In 1975, the rosette virus struck the groundnut crop of Hausaland and replanting with inferior varieties has prevented the growth of exports. In addition, the oil boom has caused some northern farmers to abandon export crops in favour of food crops such as maize, for which there is a ready market and higher prices in the cities.

The rush to the cities stimulated by the oil boom has also deprived rural areas of much of their labour and shortages have been felt particularly badly at peak periods. Southern tree crop farmers have suffered severe labour shortages at harvest, a factor which has contributed to reduced production for export. The north did not escape the labour shortage, and a common sight was cotton fields which were past their best but which had not yet been harvested due to lack of labour.

Since Nigeria's economy has long been based on the export of agricultural raw materials, one is tempted to associate severe decline in agricultural exports with severe decline in the agricultural sector. This is not necessarily so, for although agriculture has had its share of problems, the trend in agricultural exports clearly exaggerates the case. As with most statistics, these need to be treated with caution and examined in conjunction with other indicators.

Import statistics

If, as has been suggested, exports are falling and farmers are oriented more towards meeting their own needs, one would expect imports of foodstuffs to fall as well. On the contrary, Nigeria's food imports soared from the mid 1970s, increasing faster than all other import categories. Figure 4 shows the rise in imports

Figure 4   Trends in some of Nigeria's imports

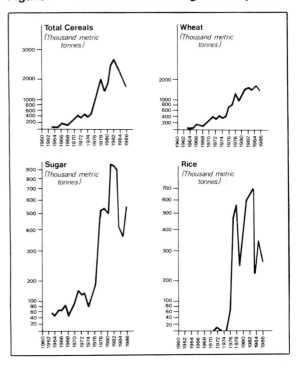

of selected food products. In 1971, food imports cost Nigeria $130 million and represented 8.6 per cent of total imports. By 1981–82, they had reached $1794 million, 14.2 per cent of the total value of imports (Watts and Bassett, 1984). With the problems facing the agricultural sector, it was no real surprise that by the mid 1970s agricultural output had fallen and there were food shortages. The government stepped in to meet the shortfall with imports but this stop-gap measure soon became a permanent feature. Imports were largely destined for the urban population. As the urban population grew, the tastes of the original urban dwellers were soon adopted by the new migrants. Traditional staples gave way to supposedly more sophisticated foods such as rice, dairy products and bread. It was these, or the raw materials necessary for their manufacture, that were imported.

With the abundance of oil money in the mid 1970s, paying for imports was no problem. Also, imports were particularly attractive at this time as they were relatively cheap. Domestic inflation grew rapidly as foreign exchange from the oil boom flooded the Nigerian economy and this reduced the value of the naira (the domestic currency) at home. Table 2 and Figure 5 show how the real exchange rate of the naira tripled in the 11 years to 1977, making goods traded in Nigeria (food in particular) much more expensive than imports. In contrast, the purchasing power of the currency remained strong on the international market because it was backed by oil. Therefore, imports continued to enter Nigeria cheaply even when prices of domestically produced and traded commodities were rising (Figure 5). Private contractors and merchants rushed to obtain import licences from the government as this not only gave them access to valuable foreign exchange but also enabled them to make vast profits from cheap imports which fetched very high prices on the urban black market.

Table 2   Nigerian exchange rates

Year	Official exchange rate ($ per naira)	Real exchange rate (1968 = 1)
1968	1.40	1.000
1969	1.40	1.043
1970	1.40	1.122
1971	1.40	1.248
1972	1.52	1.354
1973	1.52	1.346
1974	1.62	1.455
1975	1.59	1.748
1976	1.59	2.016
1977	1.53	2.210
1978	1.54	2.578
1979	1.78	3.038

The fact that Nigeria became 'hooked' on imports was tragic for the domestic producer. Not only did demand for traditional food products decline in urban areas but, even worse, domestic agriculture lost much of the market for its products in domestic industry. Industry grew to depend on imported raw materials. It was easier to telephone suppliers in the USA for wheat or rice, for example, than to attempt to obtain supplies from ill-organised Nigerian producers whose reliability was often in question and who were lax about quality control.

At face value, import statistics imply that agriculture could not cope with demand. However, if one looks at production trends for rice and wheat, for example, they reflect a rapid rise in production which parallels the rising import pattern. Agriculture, it seems, *was* attempting to meet this new and changing demand. What the statistics do not reveal is why the agricultural sector failed in this attempt. The view of this author is that the effects of the oil boom, and resulting government policies, actually hindered agriculture in its efforts to meet the rising demand. Continued imports forced agriculture to remain in a relatively subsistence role. Prices and marketing of domestically produced crops failed to take advantage of whatever expansion was taking place in consumer demand.

Crop production statistics

If export crop production fell, and imports, particularly of foodstuffs, were too expensive for rural dwellers, one would expect an increase in subsistence crop production. Folayan (1983) assures us that this did occur, particularly in the case of crops for which

Figure 5   Trends in exchange rates

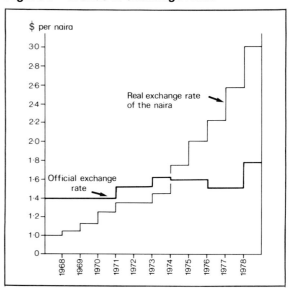

demand was high such as rice and maize. However, there is a wide margin of error in the production statistics which makes this very difficult to prove. Figures 6, 7 and 8 show the production of root crops, grains and rice based on data from several sources. The variation in these production statistics is quite dramatic. USDA and, to a lesser extent, the FAO support Folayan's view that rice production increased markedly, while data from other sources are not so conclusive. The greatest problem with food crops is that one can never be sure how much has been consumed and how much sold. Unfortunately, therefore, crop production statistics are of little value as an indicator of the state of Nigerian agriculture. One can only accept the view of those with field experience, which is that farmers, during the oil boom, did modify traditional cropping. They did this to make sure they

Figure 6 Production estimates for coarse grains

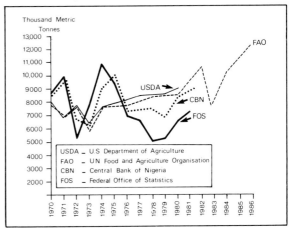

USDA – U.S Department of Agriculture
FAO – U.N Food and Agriculture Organisation
CBN – Central Bank of Nigeria
FOS – Federal Office of Statistics

Explanation of terms involved in Figure 5

Official exchange rate of the naira   This is the official exchange rate in terms of $US per naira, the rate at which central banks will exchange currencies. It is used in calculating the prices of imports and exports.

Real exchange rate of the naira   This differs from the official exchange rate because it reflects the internal purchasing power of the currency and not the artificially held official rate. The real rate of exchange is not fixed. Figure 5 shows the real exchange rate between Nigeria and the United States, for example.

The influx of foreign exchange from oil from the mid-1970s onwards meant that the value of the naira at home fell far more than it did on the international markets.

The following example shows how the prices of goods produced and traded within Nigeria rose far more between 1968 and 1979, than did the price of imported goods. It was this that made imports so attractive. (Refer to Figure 5.)

1   Impact of real exchange growth on domestic prices

If a quantity of domestically produced beans were valued at N10 (the real rate of exchange), in 1968, by 1979 they had increased in value to a level that was 3.038 times that of 1968.

Therefore, beans which were valued at N10 in 1968, would have been valued at N30.38 in 1979.

2   Impact of lesser growth of official exchange rate on import prices

If a quantity of imported rice cost US $14.0 or N10 at the official exchange rate in 1968 (see Table 2), by 1979 the rice had increased in cost by 27 per cent (1.78 ÷ 1.40)

Therefore, imported rice which cost US $14 or N10 in 1968 would have cost $17.8 or N12.7 in 1979.

3   Summary to compare relative price increases

	1968	1979
domestically grown beans	N10	N30.38
imported rice	N10	N12.7

Clearly imports were favoured.

Figure 7   Production estimates for root crops

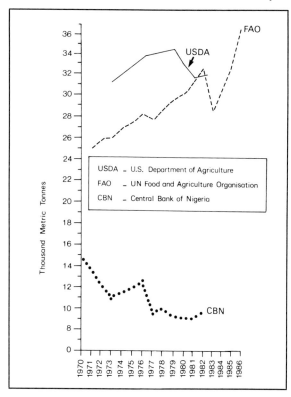

Figure 8   Rice (paddy) production estimates

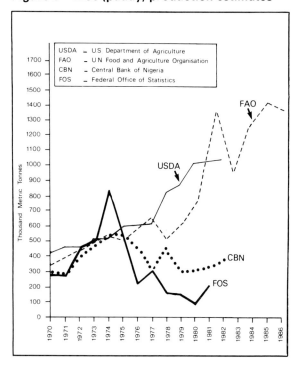

had enough food to feed themselves and to meet the demands of local markets rather than export markets.

Domestic food price levels

Nigeria's extortionate food prices of the 1970s and early 1980s are sometimes thought to be symbolic of food shortages and hence the inability of the farming sector to meet food demands. High food prices in the rural areas have often reflected the harsh times which followed periodic droughts, mainly in the north, and bush fires and disease throughout the country. Local food shortages resulting from such problems have led to price increases. But what caused high food prices in Nigeria's urban areas?

The influx of money from the sale of oil led to rapid inflation at home, with food and other goods produced in Nigeria costing much more. Collier (1983) estimated that between 1968 and 1977 food prices rose by 170 per cent compared to non-food prices. However, because Nigeria's wealth was based on oil, which the international financial markets regarded as a guarantee of economic success, the Nigerian currency, the naira, actually increased its value against other currencies. This made imports cheaper and hit domestic production very hard.

Tremendous demand for imported goods followed. Food imports were controlled by traders who were able to hoard food and obtain artificially high prices because they had a monopoly over its distribution. Thus in the early 1980s, 50 kg of imported rice with a wholesale value of $52 was being sold at over $180.

Calorie consumption

According to World Bank statistics, Nigerians were consuming an average of 2022 calories each day in 1983, 86 per cent of the recommended calorie intake. If the availability of food had been sufficient to meet demand, this figure would surely have been higher. In reality, the situation in the rural areas was, and probably is, more serious than statistics suggest. The urban rich almost certainly have more than their fair share of food, while the poor urban dweller, with only marginal employment, and the rural dweller have much less to eat.

Summary

Since independence, agriculture has suffered relative, though not necessarily absolute, decline. Total farm output has increased though not on a per capita basis. Numerous factors have contributed to this situation and in the next chapter we shall examine some of these.

Assignments

1 (a) Explain why the production of export crops declined in Nigeria after independence.
   (b) Why did cotton and groundnut production fall so dramatically after 1972?
   (c) Why might the trends in exports overstate the decline in the agricultural sector as a whole?
2 (a) Using Figure 4, calculate the percentage increase in imports of sugar and rice after 1974.
   (b) Analyse the economic and social factors responsible for the rise in imports of agricultural products in the 1970s.
3 Why is it so difficult to establish the real trends in agricultural production in Nigeria?

Questions from A level examination papers

4 Describe and account for the distribution and changing regional and national importance in West Africa of any two of the following commercial crops: oil palm, groundnuts, cocoa, cotton. (Oxford, June 1985)
5 (a) In what different ways may agricultural regions be identified and delimited?
   (b) With the help of a sketch-map, divide a country or major region you have studied into agricultural regions and explain the criteria you have used. (Cambridge, November/December 1984)

2
Causes of agricultural decline

Several factors are responsible for decline in the agricultural sector. In this chapter we shall concentrate on two major variables which have influenced the agricultural sector in Nigeria, oil and government policy.

The impact of oil

Background to the oil boom

Commercial production of oil began in Nigeria in 1957, after some 20 years of exploration by a consortium of Royal Dutch Shell and British Petroleum. At this stage no-one appreciated how extensive the oil reserves would prove to be. Things really started to move when an oil exporting terminal was built at Bonny and linked to oil fields both nearby and across the Niger River in what is now Bendel State. Offshore reserves were exploited next and production moved ahead rapidly, hesitating only during the Nigerian civil war (1967–70). After the conflict, production rose sharply and by 1979 reached a maximum of 2.3 million barrels per day (bpd) (Table 3). Production was never to go higher than this but with the manoeuvring of OPEC (of which Nigeria was a member), prices soared (Figure 9) and so did Nigeria's foreign exchange earnings. By 1980, oil was contributing over 90 per cent of foreign exchange.

There was evidence of Nigeria's new-found wealth everywhere in the urban areas by the early 1970s: new roads, new buildings, people in new cars, new hospitals, schools, institutions of higher education. Accompanying this wealth was a common belief that Nigeria had at last found a way out of poverty. By contrast, the rural areas remained markedly unchanged.

Substantial oil price increases throughout the 1970s (Figure 9) helped to generate a feeling that a permanent source of wealth had been found. By 1978/79, Nigeria had overspent its resources on imports, many of which proved unproductive. For example, international banks encouraged Nigeria to accept loans (on which interest had to be paid) for development of the infrastructure, and foreigners were quite unscrupulous about selling expensive equipment and materials to Nigeria which were really of little use. British Aerospace sold Nigeria war planes it did not need. The USSR was instrumental in the establishment of a steel plant on the Niger River, miles from anywhere. Ten years after it was started, the plant is still nowhere near completion and has cost Nigeria a great deal of money.

Table 3 Nigerian oil production

Year	Million barrels per day
1978	1.9
1979	2.3
1980	2.1
1981	1.4
1982	1.3
1983	1.2
1984	1.4
1985	1.4

Figure 9   Nigerian light crude official prices

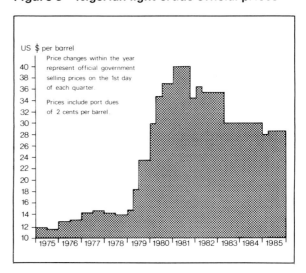

The only thing that saved Nigeria's economy towards the end of the 1970s was another massive increase in oil prices. While output of oil remained more or less constant, revenue again increased dramatically in 1979–80 (Figure 9), so Nigeria's income rose to match her spending.

However, oil had priced itself out of the market, and by 1981 demand and prices started to fall. Output, too, was reduced by quotas, and revenue from oil fell sharply. The debt that Nigeria had incurred as she overspent had now become a major problem. While banks and others to whom loans were due were tolerant at first, they ceased to be so in 1983 when Nigeria's shortage of foreign exchange became acute. Nigeria did little to curb foreign spending and under the civilian ruler President Shagari, even selective import controls were abolished. The crisis contributed to Shagari's downfall and, by the end of 1983, the economy was in total chaos.

Since this time Nigeria has had two military governments but it was only under the regime of President Babangida that a more positive approach to Nigeria's problems was taken. Since the fall in oil prices to less than $10 a barrel in 1986, revenue has been even lower than was anticipated. This makes it all the more important that President Babangida's policies for diversifying the economy succeed.

After this brief history of the oil industry, we now go on to examine some of the effects of oil on the rural sector.

Oil, a cause of rural–urban migration

Rural–urban migration is not new to Nigeria. However, as people became aware of the employment opportunities provided by the oil industry, they left their homes and farms for the 'streets of gold' in the cities. In most cases only a few family members migrated but sometimes entire families abandoned their farms for city life.

Underemployment is a common problem for much of the year in rural Nigeria, but at times of peak activity, when fields are being prepared for sowing, when the bush is cleared for new fields, and particularly at harvest time, labour is always in demand. The race from rural to urban areas, stimulated by the oil industry, left agriculture short of labour during these peak periods.

According to the World Bank, the proportion of workers in the agricultural sector has declined from around 72 per cent of the population in 1965, to around 67 per cent in 1980. In spite of the proportionate decrease, the number of workers in the rural areas

is thought to have remained constant owing to population increase. This has not benefited agriculture as one might expect. In reality, there are now more of the 'wrong sort' of workers in rural areas. The most able, the young men and women, have migrated, leaving the working population heavily weighted towards the very old and the very young. There may not be a general shortage of labour in rural Nigeria but acute shortages at peak periods are a problem for those left on the farms.

Although crop production statistics indicate that total output from the farm sector has continued to rise, this is only an average situation for the country as a whole. In many areas drought and disease have struck as well. This, combined with low producer prices, the effects of inflation and a shortage of labour at crucial periods, has resulted in decreased production in some regions. Where such conditions prevail and the number of dependants on the farm remains the same or is even greater than before, hardship can be extreme.

Furthermore, with the end of the oil boom, employment prospects have declined in the urban areas and many who once found employment on the fringes of the oil industry (in related service industries, for example) are suffering. As shortages in both domestic and imported food have forced prices to rise, it is the unskilled migrants from the rural areas who have suffered especially. They no longer have the capacity to produce their own food but do not have the resources to pay the high prices that reserve food for the moneyed classes. One result is that, in times of stress, those suffering in the urban areas return to their villages, putting additional pressure on rural areas where per capita food production is lower than it was.

How oil accelerated rural decline

The introduction of cash crops, which began in the early 19th century, revolutionised the economy and in many ways had as much effect as oil, even though it was more gradual. The flow of money into the economy reached a wide range of people: from farmers to traders and other middle-men/women involved in the export process. Even if the distribution of this new income was uneven, it did reach both the rural and the urban areas.

In contrast, the oil money has been channelled mainly through the Federal and State governments and has been concentrated in towns and cities, not in rural areas. Policies designed to stimulate agriculture were started as long ago as the early 1970s but their success was limited. Oil revenues could have been invested in agriculture to greater effect, but this was not done. Instead, most went into the urban areas as politicians were more sensitive to urban demands than to rural ones. Some of the oil wealth was used to buy new machinery for farms, usually by family members who had migrated to the cities. Apart from this, the majority of rural Nigerians hardly benefited at all.

How food consumption patterns changed with oil wealth

The change in patterns of food consumption was mentioned earlier. How it came about and its effect on agriculture are considered below. One must try to imagine the change in lifestyle for the rural–urban migrant. In rural areas there are periods of hectic activity when the whole family/village is involved in the fields. The men work predominantly in the fields. The women work in the fields as well, but also do the housework, look after the children and the vegetable gardens, cultivate their own plots, and market their own goods and those produced by others. In addition to all these activities there is the cooking. This is a lengthy chore which, in the south, involves pounding maize, yam, or other root crops and, in the north, making couscous from millet.

Once rural migrants became urban residents, whether in a house or a shanty town, they lost the immediate support of the extended village family. The migrants had to do everything for themselves, including the cooking. Not all the migrants were men. Women migrants who had to work, now prepared quicker dishes rather than the labour intensive foods. People no longer had the time to prepare traditional cereal dishes and tastes changed. Rice developed a previously unknown popularity because it had the prestige of being an 'upmarket' food used by the urban elite and because it was quick to cook. Dairy produce increased

An Ibadan market, typically dominated by women traders

in popularity too, and bread, yet another staple of the urban areas, was adopted throughout the country.

This change in taste meant that Nigerians were increasingly eating foodstuffs that were not produced in adequate quantities by Nigerian farmers. As domestic food production was not meeting demand, it appeared that there was a food shortage. In fact the nature of demand for food had changed.

How oil-based inflation affected farming

Nigeria's inflation rate raced upwards once the impact of oil wealth was felt. Prices for most goods rose, as did wages, though farm prices were held down by the government. The farmer's position actually became less competitive. Consumer goods, farm implements and inputs cost much more, but farm produce was sold for much the same price. Being self-employed, the farmer was unable to benefit directly from wage increases, though hired labour cost a great deal more. Scarcity of labour owing to migration to the urban areas inflated the level of wages. Moreover, knowledge of how much others were earning in the non-farm sector kept rural wages high. With limited political influence, it seemed that the farmer simply could not win. The fall in the value of the naira at home (Figure 5 and Table 2) and the stimulus given to imports by the international strength of the currency, meant that Nigeria relied increasingly on cheap imported supplies. Her own producers could not compete. Oil generated high levels of inflation which helped to make the rich much richer and the poor poorer, particularly in the urban areas.

Government policy on agriculture

Adverse government policies soon after independence

After independence in 1960, the Nigerian government decided to pursue a policy of industrialisation aimed at replacing imports with goods produced in Nigeria. This new industrialisation was financed by export taxes. As agricultural raw materials were Nigeria's chief exports, it was therefore the farm sector that effectively subsidised industrialisation. As the years passed, the burden of taxation increased, leaving the farmer poorer. Farmers were subjected not only to taxes on their export products but also to import duties on consumer goods and to poll taxes

(taxes paid by all adults). These severe demands on a farmer's income lowered morale in the farming sector and had a damaging effect on cash cropping (Berry, 1975). While manufacturing increased its contribution to the nation's gross domestic product (Figure 2), agriculture's contribution to GDP had already fallen by 1970, before the impact of oil had really been felt.

Government policy on agriculture, 1970–1985

1970 saw the end of the Nigerian civil war and the beginning of major changes in Nigeria's economy. The fall in agricultural exports was becoming increasingly apparent. Even though problems in the rural sector attracted far less interest than the oil boom, changes intended to stimulate agriculture were nonetheless taking place.

Restructuring the marketing boards

The marketing boards were established in the colonial era. Their original aim was to secure the production of agricultural raw materials for export. Farmers were offered a fixed price for their crops. The fact that income was guaranteed, as long as the crop was harvested, gave farmers security against fluctuating prices in the market place. The disadvantage was that the fixed price was always below the price paid by traders, so the boards were doing farmers a disservice (Table 4). At this time the farmer had no alternative

but to sell to the commodity marketing board. Farmers could, and very often did, sell on the black market but for the most part they were trapped into selling at the lower price.

In 1973 the government decided to restructure the marketing boards to give farmers a better deal. Taxes were reduced and producer prices shot up from 1973–74, the situation being furthered by buoyant export prices. In 1977 there were further reforms. The marketing boards ceased to be state operated and were replaced by a national board for each commodity. These were established for cocoa, groundnuts, palm produce, cotton and rubber. Previously rubber had not been subject to a marketing board regime. Grains, tubers and root crops also came under the system. In the case of crops for the domestic market (food crops) the boards were to purchase any surplus, thus guaranteeing a fixed price for any crop that was left unsold. Hopefully, the farmer would have achieved a higher price on the open market for the bulk of the crop. In this way it was hoped to stimulate production of domestic food crops and export crops.

Why restructuring the marketing boards was not successful

As the data reveal, there has not been a revival of export crops. One of the main reasons for this was that the price increases in the mid 1970s were not sustained. As Table 5 shows, prices for palm kernels remained at N150 per tonne from 1975–78. Groundnut prices rose from N250 to N275 per tonne during the same period. Cocoa remained constant at N660 per tonne until 1977, when it shot up to N1030. In few cases between 1975 and 1978 did price increases match the rise in inflation. Price rises continued in the 1980s, though once again they were insufficient to reverse the downward export trend.

Problems faced by tree crop farmers

The major earners of export revenue in Nigeria have traditionally been the tree crops of the south. For these there is a long time between planting and harvesting. Government policy did stimulate some renewed planting but on the whole it was limited. By

Table 4   Comparison of marketing board and traders' prices

	Marketing board prices 1982–1983 (naira per tonne)	Farm gate prices paid by traders 1982–1983 (naira per tonne)
Beans	362	810
Maize	210	580
Millet	231	330
Sorghum	220	340
Paddy rice	400	550
Milled rice	596	not available

Table 5   Producer prices* for export crops

	1974/75	75/76	76/77	77/78	81/82	82/83	83/84	84/85	85/86
Palm kernels	124	150	150	150	200	230	230	230	230
Groundnuts	145	250	250	275	450	450	450	650	750
Cocoa beans	487	660	660	1030	1300	1300	1425	1500	1600
Seed cotton	156	308	308	330	431	431	560	700	850

* producer prices are marketing board or fixed prices

the late 1970s, tree crop farmers were facing other problems too. Many cocoa farmers in particular had committed themselves so heavily to cocoa that they had left themselves short of food crops. Up until the 1960s, returns from cocoa were good, and even in subsequent years when profits fell it was still better to produce cocoa than to be heavily dependent on subsistence farming. Indeed, as returns fell, many cocoa growers expanded their crop at the expense of subsistence crops and bought in food from outside the region. However, in the 1960s, there was a decline in replanting and a high proportion of cocoa trees are now old, diseased and well past their best bearing years. Also, the cost of harvesting the crop has escalated with the rising cost of labour. Together with the increase in food prices and the general effects of inflation, these factors have left many cocoa farmers much poorer in real terms.

With the government's emphasis on industrialisation since independence, the domestic demand for many products has increased. Palm oil and rubber producers in particular have found an industrial outlet for their crops. They have not been trapped in quite the same way as the cocoa producers.

Why the north did not respond to changes in the marketing boards
In the north, restructuring the marketing boards should have had a more immediate impact as annual field crops predominate there. Instead, the farmers seem to have turned to subsistence crops or food crops such as rice and maize rather than export crops such as groundnuts and cotton. Market demand for these subsistence crops was substantial, and the prices paid by traders were far in excess of marketing board prices (Table 4). The government's scheme of restructuring the marketing boards had clearly failed and under President Babangida the boards were abolished in 1986.

The 1970s, an era of large-scale agricultural projects

Irrigation projects
Under the third five year plan (1975–80), agriculture was given a relatively high priority and it was during this era that Nigeria launched into large-scale irrigation. Irrigation had been introduced on a small scale in the 1950s but by 1968 irrigation of rice (mainly in the Niger region) and wheat in the far north was only 13,000 hectares. These irrigation schemes were not without problems but these appear to have been overlooked as Nigeria enthusiastically set up large-scale schemes with much encouragement

from international agencies and consultants. The potential for rice and wheat was judged to be considerable. Irrigation schemes were soon under way which aimed to cover a total of around 60,000 hectares in the southern Lake Chad region, in the Kano River valley and the Sokoto-Rima valley.

By 1980 there were eleven River Basin Development Authorities (RBDAs) in Nigeria, all involved in irrigated farming. However, the problems associated with these have been numerous. There has been resistance from the people living in the area and the schemes have been far more costly and far less successful than anticipated (Table 6). The case study in Chapter 4 examines the Kano River scheme in some detail.

Table 6 **Planned and actual investment costs of large scale irrigation projects in the north**

| Project | Investment costs (N/ha)* | |
	Plan estimate	Apparent/Actual
Sokoto phase I	6400	13,500
Kano phase I	4200	5100–7400
South Chad phase I	4300	7600–10,500

* All costs and returns estimated on a 1979 basis.

The agricultural development projects
Running parallel with the River Basin Development Authorities were the integrated Agricultural Development Projects (ADPs). Funding for these came predominantly from the World Bank and also from federal and state funds. These schemes aimed to help the small farmer by developing (i) local technology which would provide seed, fertiliser, insecticides and pesticides (ii) an infrastructure which the farmer could use: roads, dams, irrigation canals, extension services, credit facilities and a marketing structure. The area covered by the ADPs and the number of farmers involved in the programmes were far greater than in the irrigation projects. Nigeria's earliest ADPs were located in the north at Funtua, Gombe and Gusau. Based on their achievements, ADPs have been extended to the middle belt and the south and there are now seventeen of them (see Figure 10). The case study in Chapter 5 examines Lafia ADP in the middle belt. ADPs have also had their problems — ecological, managerial, social and economic. However, ADPs have not created the same physical disruption as the large-scale irrigation projects. The farmers remain the main decision makers on their farms and can either participate in the development projects or not.

Figure 10   Agricultural Development Projects

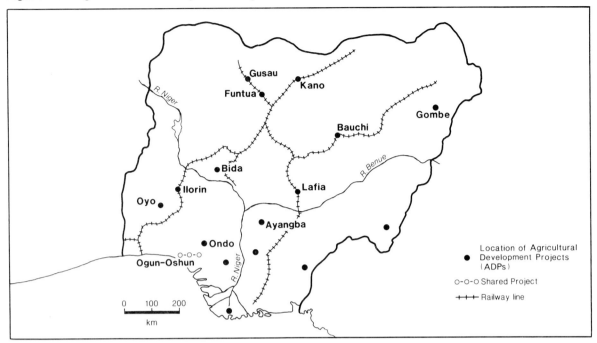

It is this relative freedom that has appealed to Nigerians. Even though the Babangida government has now phased out its direct involvement in agricultural production, it still permits the ADPs to provide extension services and other help to farmers (*African Business*, March 1987, p. 56).

Associated with the RBDAs and the ADPs have been national schemes to give farmers credit facilities and supplies of fertiliser. However, like all the other schemes, these started well but their level of success then declined.

Large-scale capital-intensive farms
A scheme initiated under the third five year plan which is still being encouraged is the development of large-scale capital-intensive farming. Initially such schemes were government run but more recently there has been increasing emphasis on privately run schemes: anything from 50 to 20,000 hectares. Large areas of the north have been taken over for such large-scale private schemes. These produce irrigated maize. The success rate has been relatively high. Some large farms in northern Nigeria have successfully provided employment for local smallholders but there is often strong opposition from the traditional farmer. One of the problems associated with large-scale farming is how to acquire the necessary land. However, the Land Use Decree of 1978 transferred

all land to state ownership and since then the state has been able to allocate land considered unused or under used to large-scale enterprises. In spite of this, acquiring land rights still takes a considerable length of time and there is usually strong opposition by local communities.

The current government is trying to encourage local industry to use raw materials grown in Nigeria rather than to import them. Large farms are attractive to industrialists because they make it easier to guarantee supplies. However, development of large farms may cause considerable conflict with the smallholder who will lose his domestic industrial market. As yet, foreigners cannot own land but Nigerian-foreign partnerships are being encouraged to seek leases for large areas of farm land. Many crops have been tried but the most popular at present is irrigated maize which yields a variety of by-products. Oil palm plantations are being encouraged in the south and sugar production could increase, particularly as the government has announced a ban on sugar imports from 1989. Whether Nigeria will be self-sufficient in sugar production by this time is, however, doubtful.

The prospects for large-scale capital-intensive farming are at present bright. However, in spite of the Babangida regime's commitment to helping the smallholder, the success of large-scale capital-intensive farming could create major problems for such farmers.

15

Specific initiatives

Since 1970, several initiatives have been introduced to bring new technology to the small farmer. These schemes are in addition to the ADPs and RBDAs. Although their methods of operation have varied, the objective of self-sufficiency in food has remained the same.

The National Accelerated Food Production Programme In 1973, the National Accelerated Food Production Programme (NAFPP) was launched. This concentrated on the distribution to smallholders of packages of information and raw materials designed to improve the production of wheat, sorghum, millet, rice, maize and cassava. To ensure that farmers were able to use the packages, a dense network of extension workers and agro-service centres was set up. In theory the scheme had much to offer, but in practice it was of limited benefit as the government ceased to contribute adequate funds and the system collapsed.

Operation Feed the Nation In 1976, unnerved by the vast amounts of foreign exchange leaving Nigeria to pay for increasing quantities of imports, the government introduced Operation Feed the Nation (OFN). This was a hurried initiative which was not clearly thought out by a regime anxious to keep the urban and student population content. Once again, the objective, as the name suggests, was self-sufficiency in food. Subsidised supplies of fertilisers, seeds, insecticides and pesticides, among other items, were provided. The media urged everyone to cultivate their back gardens intensively and to keep chickens, whose eggs and meat would provide an important source of protein and whose droppings could be used as fertiliser. The necessary supplies were to be distributed by thousands of students who were paid to do this during their long vacation. However, success was limited as some two-thirds of the entire government allocation in the first year of the OFN programme was spent on student wages, leaving little for the farmer. Supplies were not sustained and efforts were subsequently concentrated on the establishment of OFN farms rather than on smallholders.

The Green Revolution In 1983, with the return of civilian rule under Shehu Shagari, the remains of OFN were cancelled and replaced with a much more ambitious and highly organised system run by the National Council for the Green Revolution. It was operated on Green Revolution principles, that is, the use of high yielding varieties of seed, high inputs of fertiliser, irrigation, etc. The new system offered renewed hope for farmers but like its predecessors, this too failed through bureaucratic problems. The

people in senior administrative positions had little or no connection with those working in the field. In this post oil boom period, as Nigeria's foreign exchange crisis deepened, the government became less and less willing to spend money on the agricultural sector.

The approaches to developing Nigerian agriculture have not been lacking in imagination. In almost every case, however, success has been minimal because the government has failed to maintain its investment in agriculture.

Agricultural policies under Babangida, 1985 to the present

General Babangida assumed power following a military coup on 27 August 1985. His objectives, stated in the 1986 budget, were essentially to restructure and diversify the productive base of the economy to make Nigeria less dependent on oil and foreign imports.

In agriculture, a series of radical measures have been adopted to increase production and several imports have now been banned, including rice, maize, day old chicks, stock fish and vegetable oil. Imports of raw materials which could be produced in Nigeria are to be banned from January 1989. This will affect many aspects of domestic industry including brewing, the manufacture of soft drinks, flour milling, baking, textile manufacture and the production of vegetable oil. The country is capable of producing the necessary raw materials but it remains to be seen whether production and storage of agricultural produce can be organised by January 1989. While imports are being restricted, exports are being encouraged. The government has pledged support for the small farmer. Aspects of the infrastructure which would benefit rural areas, such as road and other transport networks, are to be developed.

The marketing boards have been abolished, so producers no longer have low prices forced upon them. Much needed credit is also to be more readily available to smallholders.

A major achievement of the Babangida government is the adjustment it has achieved in the exchange rate. A second tier foreign exchange market was established in September 1986. This has allowed foreign currencies to be auctioned in Nigerian cities for certain aspects of trade. Through this the true value of the naira has emerged and the system has achieved an effective devaluation of the currency by some 60 per cent. The process was something that many previous governments had shrunk from but it has been swift and successful. It will also help producers of export crops as Nigeria's exports will now be cheaper on the world market. Conversely, imports will be dearer.

Although the discussion here focuses on agriculture, it is important to note that many of the austerity measures adopted by the Babangida government are very similar to the Structured Adjustment Programmes (SAPs) imposed by the IMF on other West African nations. The government has thus received a fairly positive reception from the West.

Agriculture has a brighter future now than it has had since independence and hopes are high following good harvests in 1985 and 1986. However, four problems are still outstanding. First, in spite of the government's commitment to smallholders, the encouragement being given to large-scale capitalist farming for the production of raw materials for industry could severely affect small farmers, particularly in the area of domestic industry. Secondly, while the abolition of the marketing boards was accepted with enthusiasm, there is now no clear structure to replace them and no guidance has been given on how private traders should operate to prevent further exploitation of the producer. Thirdly, the Babangida regime started with great

popular support but many of its policies, such as salary cuts for the civil service, have hit hardest at those who are most powerful. Continued political stability is essential if the policies being undertaken by the government are to be carried through effectively. Finally, Nigeria's debt is rising. At $26 billion it is the highest in West Africa. Foreign leaders are increasingly reluctant to invest in Nigeria. A reduction in the supply of investment capital could hinder the policies designed to stimulate the rural sector. Whether foreign investment will be revived if Nigeria's economy shows positive signs of recovery as a result of internal financial controls, remains to be seen.

Summary

The rising importance of oil in Nigeria's economy and the failure of government policy to provide a stable framework within which oil revenues could be used for rural development have both contributed to agricultural failures. Nigerian governments have always considered agriculture to be of secondary importance. Changes in both the traditional and modern types of agriculture have to be seen in the context of this post-independence political framework.

Assignments

1 Using Table 3 and Figure 9, calculate Nigeria's total annual income from oil production in the years 1978 to 1985. When was the peak of revenue reached? Why has the revenue declined since then?

2 Draw a flow chart to illustrate the effects of the oil boom on the agricultural sector. (Pay special attention to the effects on the labour force, on consumption patterns, and on relative prices of imports and exports.)

3 Discuss the reasons for and the effects of government policy towards agricultural prices in Nigeria.

4 How has the government of Nigeria sought to increase agricultural output on: (a) smallholdings (b) larger scale units?

5 What was the prime cause of the failure of government initiatives in agriculture?

6 What are the problems currently facing the government of Nigeria in attempting to improve agricultural production?

Questions from A level examination papers

7 (a) Describe and account for the regional variations in agricultural land-use within Nigeria. (b) With the aid of specific examples, (i) suggest reasons for the decline in food production in Nigeria since independence (ii) describe the methods that are being used in attempts to increase agricultural output in Nigeria. (Joint Matriculation Board, June 1985)

8 With reference to one developing country, discuss those factors which hinder the improvement of agriculture. (London, January 1982)

3
Traditional farming systems

With its image of being simple, old-fashioned and backward, traditional agriculture rarely gets as much attention in the literature as do modern agricultural development projects. However, traditional farming warrants a closer look on several counts. First, the majority of Nigeria's farmers still use traditional methods and it is important to understand the way they farm. In the second place, traditional farming is not necessarily simple because it does not use sophisticated technology. On the contrary, it can be highly complex. Further study reveals the skilful adaptation of traditional farming systems to specific environments. Centuries of experience of this type of cultivation are passed on to the traditional farmer, giving him an ecological awareness. The third reason for looking in detail at traditional agriculture is that the experience of traditional systems could be used as a basis for agricultural development. This approach has been largely overlooked in Nigeria. While large-scale, modern schemes have often created environmental problems, traditional systems have long allowed the continued exploitation of the environment without its destruction. It should therefore be possible to combine the best of traditional farming, in particular the sound, underlying ecological principles, with relevant modern technology to create a suitable approach to agricultural development.

Factors affecting farming systems

The crops people grow and the animals they keep are determined by a combination of physical, social, economic and political factors. Figure 11 summarises some of the variables that influence the farming system. There are many more. The figure shows that farming systems are highly complex and do not exist in a vacuum. Important points to notice are that many of the controlling variables are inter-related and that they can operate in different directions and with different intensities in the various farming systems.

With some understanding of these controlling variables, one can generalise about farming systems on a regional basis. For instance, the physical environment broadly determines what crops can be grown, particularly in areas where the technology to modify environmental conditions is limited. Social factors such as education levels and ethnic tradition can affect who does what on the farm, whether animals are kept, and what is ultimately produced. Economic variables are numerous but factors such as market access and price to the farmer have considerable influence on what is grown. Finally, the political environment can affect farmers both directly and indirectly. An indirect effect could be via political influence on economic variables such as crop prices (Figure 11), or on social factors such as the availability of schooling or training schemes for adults. However, one variable, the climate, is of paramount importance in Nigeria and this requires detailed attention.

The climate

Many aspects of climate affect plant growth. For example, temperature, radiation and day length affect photosynthesis (the process by which green plants use sunlight to produce food). In Nigeria these factors favour plant growth but the essential element, water, is frequently inadequate. This restricts the length of the growing season and the crops that can be grown. The rainfall regime varies over the country. While much of the south receives considerable rainfall, the ecology of the northern savannas is much more fragile due to lower amounts of rainfall and its unpredictability. The causes of rainfall patterns will be discussed at a macro level as this has a fundamental influence on farming systems.

West Africa is the meeting place of two opposing air masses which originate in different source regions and so have very different characteristics. It is their relative movement which is of interest. This affects the overall climate not only of Nigeria but of the entire West African region. The more northerly is a

Figure 11 Variables influencing agriculture

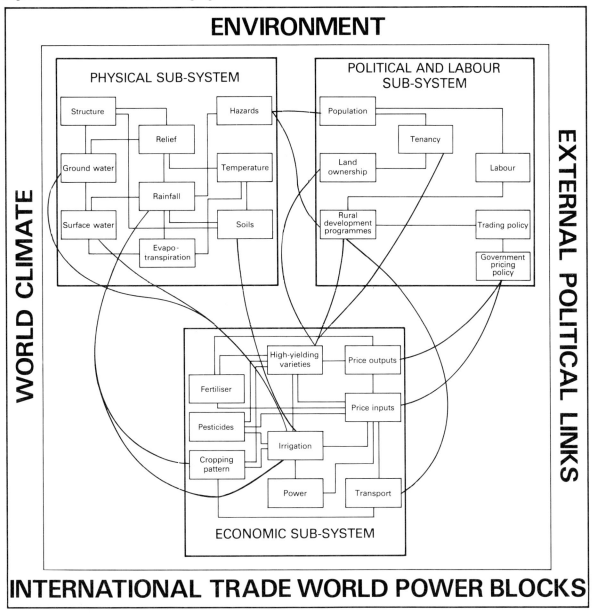

mass of warm, dry, dusty, tropical continental air blowing from the Sahara. In contrast, the more southerly mass is of warm, moist, tropical maritime air, blowing from the Atlantic Ocean on to and across the coast of West Africa. Where they meet, turbulence occurs and, given the right conditions, rainfall results. It is this frontal rainfall which determines whether there is a feast or a famine in West Africa each year.

Where the two air masses meet, the light, warm, dry air from the Sahara rides over the heavy moist maritime air, compressing it into a wedge (Figure 12,

p. 20). The sloping plane of contact between the two is known as the Intertropical Convergence Zone (ITCZ) or the Intertropical Discontinuity (ITD). Where the two air masses meet at ground level, the depth of compressed air is not sufficient to produce rain, although there may be some turbulence. Rainfall only occurs where the compressed wedge of tropical maritime air reaches a depth of some 1000–2000 m. Only then does the turbulent air rise sufficiently high to cool and so produce rain. A rainfall belt therefore occurs some 300–500 km south of the position of the ITCZ, which is at ground level. Cloud formation is

Figure 12   Diagrammatic cross section of the ITCZ over Nigeria

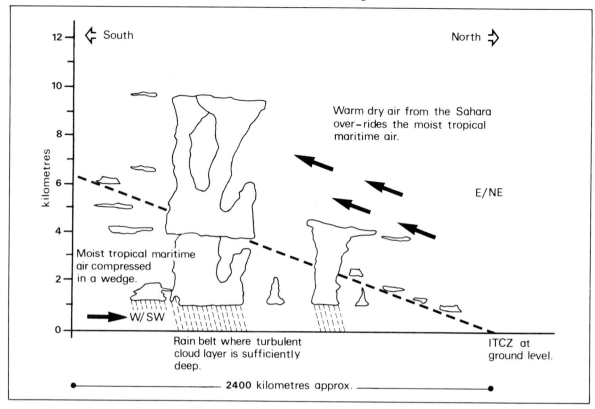

usual to the north of the rainfall belt but if the wedge of moist air is not sufficiently deep to allow adequate cooling in the upper layers, rain does not fall. It is for this reason that rolling clouds frequently bring hope but no rain to the northern savannas and the semi-arid *sahel* of the region.

Being part of the global atmospheric system, the two air masses over West Africa are never static. From December to February, when the wind belts occupy their most southerly position, the ITCZ is also furthest south, lying roughly parallel with the West African coast and 5–7° inland from it (Figure 13). By July/August, the winds and the ITCZ have migrated northwards. At its most northerly extreme the ITCZ reaches 17–21°N of The Equator, well beyond Nigeria's northern border which is approximately 14°N. With the rain belt some 300–500 km south of the ITCZ, northern Nigeria receives all of its rain as the ITCZ approaches its most northerly position.

After this it begins to move southward again. The rains are therefore restricted to the period from May to October in the north, the rest of the year being arid (Figure 14). In the south, rain falls over a longer period and there are two rainfall maxima each year, the first as the rains move north across the country

and the second as they move south. Other factors such as local relief and the effect of the sea also influence the rainfall regime in the south. However, it is the movement of the frontal system which determines rainfall patterns over the country as a whole.

Figure 15 superimposes isohyets on a vegetation map and the similarity in the patterns is at once apparent. In the far north east, the 500 mm isohyet more or less coincides with the junction between *sahel* (sub-desert) and Sudan savanna. The greater part of the country is savanna — as far south as the 1500 mm isohyet. Within this, a major transition occurs from the relatively arid Sudan savanna in the north to the greener Guinea savannas of the middle belt, where grassland and forest intermingle. South of the 1500 mm isohyet, the forest becomes increasingly dense, culminating in the rainforest where rainfall is in excess of 3000 mm. However, little of the original rainforest now remains.

Figure 15   Rainfall in relation to vegetation

Figure 13 The ITCZ

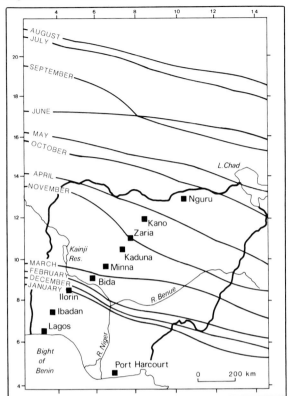

Figure 14 Annual rainfall distribution

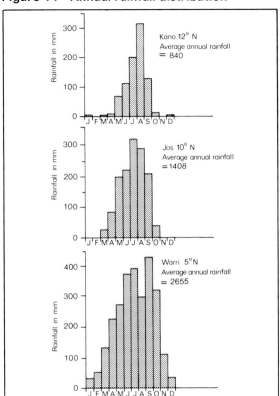

Kano 12° N
Average annual rainfall
= 840

Jos 10° N
Average annual rainfall
= 1408

Warri 5° N
Average annual rainfall
= 2655

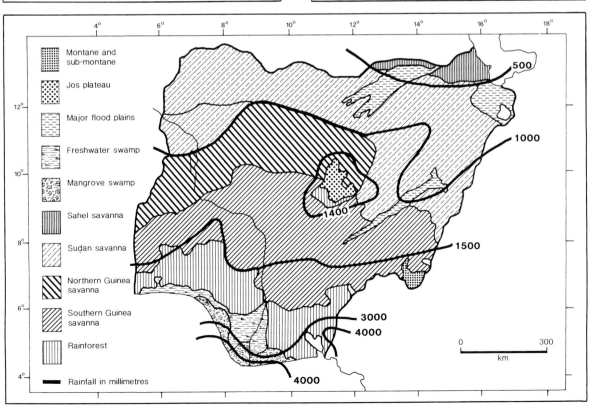

Montane and
sub-montane

Jos plateau

Major flood plains

Freshwater swamp

Mangrove swamp

Sahel savanna

Sudan savanna

Northern Guinea
savanna

Southern Guinea
savanna

Rainforest

Rainfall in millimetres

Farming systems

For convenience, Nigeria will be divided according to convention into the north, the middle belt and the south, and the farming systems in each will be examined.

The north

Lying mainly between 10°N and Nigeria's northern border (approximately 14°N), the north includes the states of Sokoto, Kano and Katsina, Kaduna State north of the town of Kaduna, and the northern part of Bauchi State north east of the Jos Plateau (Figure 16). In this Hausa-speaking area, the Hausa and settled Fulani cultivate the land and the nomadic Fulani graze their herds. The north eastern corner of Nigeria is the home of the Kanuri peoples and the heart of the ancient empire of Bornu. Fulani pastoralists are much in evidence here too. The Hausa, Fulani and Kanuri are not the only ethnic groups in the region but they outnumber the others.

The north is characterised by extensive plains ranging from 300 to 900 m above sea level. The monotony of the landscape is broken by a scatter of inselbergs, occasional hills and wide valleys. There are few permanent rivers. In the more remote areas of Bornu, the aridity of the southern *sahel* is reflected in the thorn scrub and acacia vegetation (Figure 16). The soils are grey-brown and sandy, and the air is often dust-laden as the Harmattan blows southwards from the desert, covering everything and everybody with a fine grey dust. As the *sahel* merges into the Sudan savannas of the north, the landscape becomes noticeably greener. Towards the southern edge of the Sudan savanna (roughly coincident with the southern edge of Nigeria's northern zone), grasses 1 to 1.5 m high and trees with small to medium sized leaves, including several species of acacia, are common (Hopkins, 1977) (Figure 16). An interesting man-made contrast is the very intensively cultivated, densely populated 'park farmland' round the region's large cities, in particular Sokoto and Kano. Also striking is the change in the soil as one moves southwards. Grey-brown dusty soils give way to ferruginous soils, identifiable by their intense red colour. These vary in texture, though most still have a high proportion of sand. In some areas, hard pans have formed, making these soils useless for cultivation.

While the landscape of the north varies quite considerably, the region's economy is sufficiently homogeneous to be distinguishable from the rest of the country.

1 It has a single, limited period of rainfall. This has a maximum duration of May to October in the south of the region.
2 Its agricultural systems are based on the staples millet and sorghum, on cowpeas, beans and vegetables, and on the cash crops groundnuts and cotton. There are notable variations in this pattern. In Bornu, for example, millet is the only cereal that will tolerate the aridity and sorghum is only included towards the south of the region where rainfall is heavier. Maize can be grown in the north but only towards the southern edge of the Sudan savannas where moisture levels are higher (Figure 16). Figure 17 shows the typical cropping pattern of farms in the Zaria region.
3 The third major characteristic of the northern agricultural economy is pastoralism. The nomadic Fulani are little interested in cultivation. They move their large herds of white Zebu and Fulani cattle to the south of the northern zone and into the middle belt as the dry season progresses, grazing the stubbles as they go. They return again with the advance of the rains. Their movement further south is restricted by tsetse fly, which breeds where there is bush and which, in spite of modern controls, is still a major problem for pastoralists in West Africa.

In general, the number of crops that can be grown decreases from south to north (Figure 16). This is paralleled by a corresponding increase in the number of cattle as one moves northwards. With limited and unpredictable rainfall, agriculture in the north is often difficult. However, in spite of the many environmental problems, output is still considerable. The many traditional farming techniques which are still in use are well adapted to this marginal environment. These are geared to getting the most out of the land without exhausting it.

Essentially, two types of land are farmed: upland or rainfed land and seasonally flooded land (*fadama*) in the valley bottoms. Upland farming covers by far the largest area. Every farmer cultivates rainfed land but not everyone has access to the highly-prized *fadamas* which are in relatively short supply.

Land use patterns on rainfed land in the north

The vegetable garden The most intensively cultivated land is the vegetable garden closest to the house. Here, tomatoes, onions, potatoes and a range of other vegetables are grown for household use (Figure 18). The range is far more limited in Bornu than in the Zaria region, for example, because of the shortage of water in the far north. Vegetables are usually grown

Figure 16   Agricultural land use patterns in northern Nigeria

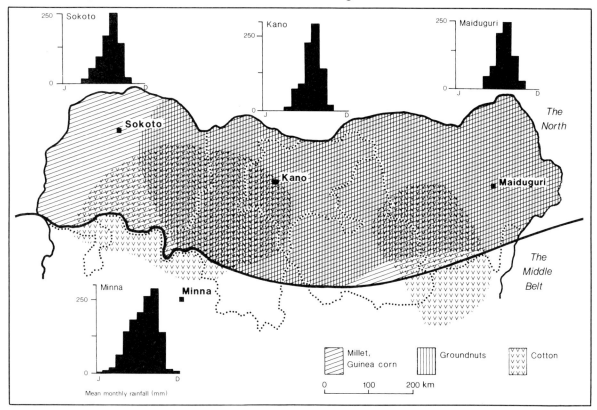

Mean monthly rainfall (mm)

Millet, Guinea corn   Groundnuts   Cotton

0   100   200 km

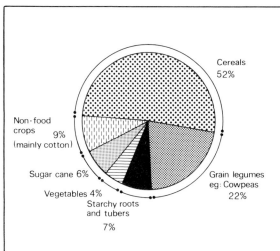

Figure 17   Typical cropping pattern of farms in the Zaria area, northern Nigeria

Cereals 52%

Non-food crops 9% (mainly cotton)

Sugar cane 6%

Vegetables 4%

Starchy roots and tubers 7%

Grain legumes eg: Cowpeas 22%

Figure 18   Village land use patterns

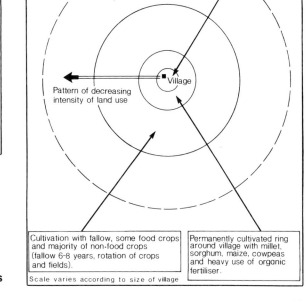

Heavy bush and limited cultivation of land : fallows much longer

Intensively cultivated compound around hut in village

Village

Pattern of decreasing intensity of land use

Cultivation with fallow, some food crops and majority of non-food crops (fallow 6-8 years, rotation of crops and fields).

Permanently cultivated ring around village with millet, sorghum, maize, cowpeas and heavy use of organic fertiliser.

Scale varies according to size of village

23

by women and are watered diligently by hand at least twice a day — water supplies permitting. This is the only involvement of most northern Nigerian women with the land, as farm work is done mainly by men. There are a few exceptions but as a rule only the poorer women work on the land.

The intensive ring of cultivation Immediately beyond the village compound is an intensively cultivated ring of rainfed land (Figure 18). Cultivation is almost continuous and in any year around 80 per cent of the fields are cropped. The staples millet and sorghum are the chief crops grown in this intensively cultivated ring but maize and cowpeas may also be grown. These tend to be the crops most needed by the household and which demand the most time. Crops requiring less attention and which in some cases do not need to be brought back to the homestead before being marketed are frequently grown further away. Cotton is one of these. The width of the intensively cultivated ring varies according to the size of the settlement. It ranges from 40 to 50 km around Sokoto and Kano (see next section and Figure 19) to the depth of a few fields around individual homesteads (Figure 18).

Figure 19 Land use pattern around urban areas of the north

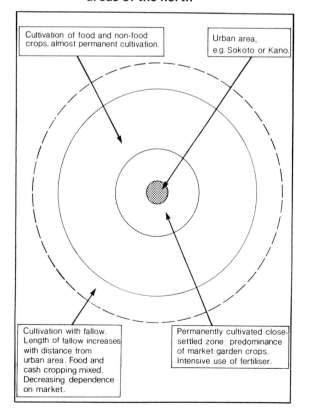

The savanna soils are relatively poor due largely to a shortage of organic matter, to leaching (nutrients being washed out of the top soil) during the rains and to erosion, mainly by wind and water. The fertility of the soil in the intensively cultivated ring is maintained by regular and frequent applications of organic material. As access to chemical fertilisers has improved, these too have been used but supplies are still far from sufficient and most of the fertiliser used is organic. The ingenious way that soil fertility is maintained in spite of limited resources deserves some discussion. Domestic refuse is composted. Dung from animals and, to a lesser extent, human excreta is collected in pit latrines. All these are used on the fields. The use of animals is significant in this part of the north. In the Zaria region, the land is farmed mainly by the Hausa and by settled Fulani who are pastoralists by tradition. The Hausa are little interested in animals and usually keep only a few donkeys, goats, sheep, chickens and ducks. The droppings from these are transported to the fields of the intensively cultivated zone in donkey carts. In contrast, the Fulani, who tend to have larger farms, own large herds of cattle which are pastured on the stubble after the harvest. This partly replenishes nutrients lost through cultivation. Further to the north west, in the Hausa dominated lands, Fulani herds are much less in evidence.

The close-settled zone around the major urban areas represents a variation on the intensively cultivated zone around villages but has slightly different characteristics due to scale (Figure 19). The close-settled zone around Sokoto is some 40 to 50 km in radius and contains within it villages, hamlets and individual farms. As around the villages, cultivation is virtually permanent within this zone, soil fertility being maintained by regular applications of composted organic refuse and by manure from small animals. As

Animals for sale at Dambarta market near Kano

in the villages, organic fertiliser is transported to the fields on donkey carts. Some chemical fertilisers are also used. Very little manure is derived from the Fulani herds in the close-settled zones around Sokoto and Kano. The herds are virtually absent here as there is little land spare for grazing.

In appearance, the land is completely clear of bush and all trees save those of economic importance such as the mango, the locust bean (*Parkia clappertoniana*) which is made into a type of cake, and the baobab (*Adansonia digitata*) the leaves of which can be used like spinach. Unlike the land under rotational bush fallow (see below), which has an untidy appearance, the close-settled zone is neat, with a scattering of trees, and is described as 'farmed parkland' (Figure 19). Cultivation of vegetables is intensive on the outskirts of the city. Every tiny patch of land is cropped and, because vegetable plots are small enough to be watered by hand, cultivation continues well into the dry season. As distance from the city increases, intensive cultivation continues as it is still worthwhile to grow crops for market but more of the staple grains and the non-food cash crops such as groundnuts and cotton appear.

Returning to Figure 11 (p. 19), it is evident that while climate dictates what staples can be grown over much of northern Nigeria, economic factors determine the land use patterns near the cities with their large market demand. Here crops are grown specifically for market rather than for subsistence as is the case in the more remote regions. It is this response to market demand which makes the intensive farming systems of the close-settled zones different from the systems in the rest of rural northern Nigeria.

Rotational bush fallow Beyond the zone of intensive cultivation is a far less intensively cultivated zone where bush fallow alternates with crops. This is a system where both crops and fields are rotated. Bush land is cleared and cultivated for several years (around five in the north). When the natural fertility of the land has been exhausted, it is left to fallow for several years, sometimes as many as 20 but usually six to eight. The untidy appearance of the landscape is deceptive. It hides the fact that most of the land is in use. The uncultivated areas are actually fallow land where the bush is in different stages of regeneration.

The system operates as follows. A patch of bush land is cleared towards the end of the dry season. All the trees which are not of economic value are cut down and the brush wood is burnt prior to the rains in May. The ash-covered land is hoed and seed is sown soon after the first rains. The rains release nutrients from the ash, particularly nitrates, and the seedlings which germinate rapidly in the high temperatures are given a considerable boost at the start of the growing season. The crop is harvested between September and October and the nutrients are replenished by herds which graze on the stubble, thus integrating pastoralism and agriculture. Apart from being grazed by animals, the land remains unused until the following March or April when the remaining stubble is burnt and the cultivation cycle is repeated (Figure 20). The cultivation cycle continues for about five years after which the land is fallowed and bush regenerates rather untidily over a period of six to eight years. This allows a gradual and natural increase in soil nutrients and fertility is restored to a considerable extent. This system of rotational bush fallow has long been

Figure 20 Main activities of the crop year: rainfed land in the north

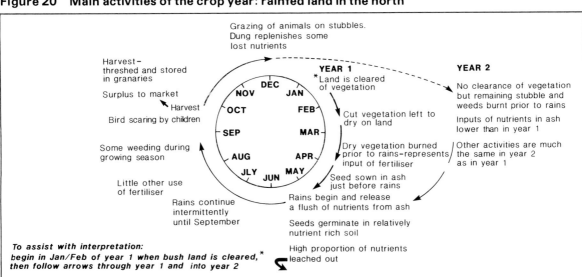

practised by traditional farmers and has permitted cultivation for centuries. In recent years the fallow period has become shorter which increases the need for fertiliser.

Traditional techniques specific to the environment

Having considered spatial differences in farming in the north and the organisation of the cropping year, this section considers the techniques used in farming. Through numerous careful farming practices, the peasant farmer is able to get the most out of relatively poor quality land without destroying it (Richards, 1985). The techniques vary in detail from one place to another but in general are to be found throughout Nigeria and are not peculiar to the north. Techniques include:

1 shallow cultivation of the land using a hoe, which keeps soil erosion to a minimum
2 the use of locally produced manure
3 bush fallowing (where the length of both the cultivation period and the fallows has been determined by generations of trial and error)
4 a detailed understanding of soil capability which results in crops being on the land best suited to them.

Intercropping and ridging are two other traditional techniques which deserve some discussion.

Intercropping is the cultivation of several different crops in the same field. This can look most untidy but there is sound ecological sense behind the apparent chaos. Intercropping is usually reserved for upland farms both in the intensively farmed zone and beyond, while the *fadamas* tend to have a higher proportion of pure stands. In his studies in northern Nigeria,

Norman (1982), identified no fewer than 178 crop combinations. The majority of farmers, however, used just ten of these, in particular the simple dual mix of millet and sorghum. It is important to note that mixed crops are not sown at random but in rows according to specific patterns (Figure 21).

The skill of the traditional cultivator ensures that mixed crops do not compete for light or for space. Crops with different growth cycles are usually grown together. Millet, for example, is sown with the first rains. It is harvested 110 days later, just when the sorghum begins to forge ahead. Research has also shown that the root positions of millet and sorghum tend to complement rather than impair each other (Norman, 1973), again reflecting the logic behind traditional techniques. Cowpeas are frequently added to the millet/sorghum crop mix and research here too has revealed the benefits of such a combination. Cowpeas are susceptible to insect damage and there is evidence that combining them with other crops reduces their vulnerability. While the yield of individual crops in mixed stands is less than the yield from a pure stand, the total return from a field is greater under mixed cropping. Furthermore, soil erosion is reduced and losses in one crop can be matched by growth in another. Finally, perhaps the greatest advantage is that both land and labour are used more efficiently under mixed cropping.

Ridging is another traditional cultivation technique usually carried out on permanently cropped, rainfed fields around the village or compound. After the dried vegetation has been burnt prior to the rains, the top soil is sometimes hoed into ridges about a metre apart and the seed sown on the ridges. This allows plants to grow in a greater depth of top soil,

Figure 21   Spatial arrangements of two common crop mixtures

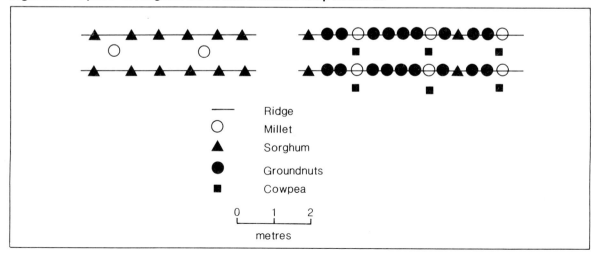

27 Ridge
Millet
Sorghum
Groundnuts
Cowpea

0   1   2

metres

Intercropping in the north

which is important on the thin savanna soils. Ridging concentrates the available nutrients around the plant roots. It also provides good drainage during the heavy rains and makes it easier to lift groundnuts as the soil is looser.

Fadama cultivation

Valley floors are known in many parts of Nigeria as *fadamas*. The water-table in these areas is relatively high and in many *fadamas* soil nutrients are replenished by annual flood water. *Fadamas* are highly prized and are usually cultivated for a longer period than rainfed land. Crops of relatively high value tend to be grown: sugar cane, rice, tomatoes and onions, for example. Techniques such as intercropping and ridging are rarely used for two main reasons. First, a crop such as sugar cane is not suited to intercropping as its height and bushiness inhibits the crops with which it is grown. Secondly, as the risk of water shortage is less in the *fadamas*, farmers prefer to grow pure stands because of the higher yields compared with mixed crops. As a rule, the labour input into the *fadamas* during the growing season is greater than into rainfed land as the financial return is much greater. This again shows how traditional farming is based on an understanding of the complex variables involved.

The middle belt

While the north has a distinctive cultural and ecological identity, the middle belt is much more difficult to define. It is roughly coincident with the ecological zone of Guinea savanna (see Figure 15, p. 21). Lying between latitude 8°N and 10½°N, it includes the states of Kwara, Benue, Niger, Plateau, Southern Kaduna, Southern Bauchi and Gongola (see Figure 22, p. 28). The most varied physical relief in Nigeria is to be found in this transitional zone. Plains ranging from below 100m above sea level in the south west of the region to around 900m south of Kaduna are dissected by the broad valleys of the Niger and the Benue rivers and also by the Gongola and part of the Kaduna river system. Generally known as Guinea savanna, the region receives rainfall for seven months of the year on average. As in the southern Sudan savannas of the north, the soils are ferruginous. Their bright red colour gives them a deceptively rich and fertile appearance.

Lying between the Sudan savanna of the north and the forested south, this region ought to be Nigeria's richest, in agricultural terms at least. Cereals from the north *and* root crops from the south can be grown here. However, it is not the richest. Many crops are

Figure 22 Agricultural land use patterns in the middle belt

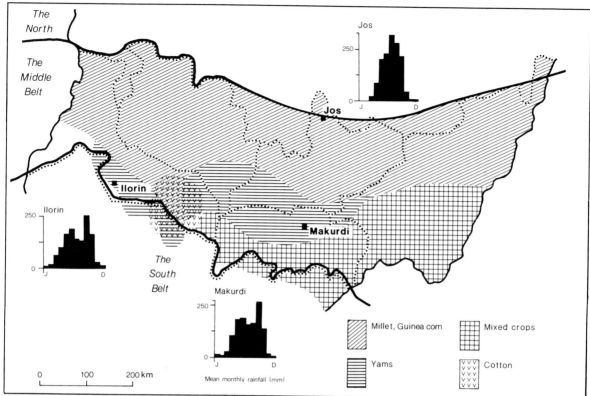

unsuccessful here, in particular the potentially valuable cash crops. Humidity levels are too low for cocoa and oil palms, the rather poor specimens of the latter being limited to the water courses. According to Morgan (1983), a major problem of the Guinea savannas is securing an adequate return to justify the cost of weeding and pest control. Cattle, an important source of revenue in the north, cannot be kept here because of tsetse fly. The only exceptions are the highland areas of the Jos Plateau and the east, and the extensively cleared areas around Shendam.

Population densities are some of the lowest in Nigeria. The middle belt occupies two-fifths of Nigeria but has only one-fifth of its people. Arguably, there are just too few people to develop the economy.

There is scope for agricultural development in the middle belt, particularly as a producer of food crops for the south. However, before much of the potentially productive land of the middle belt can be brought into use, river blindness and tsetse fly will need to be significantly reduced, if not eliminated from the region.

Land use patterns in the plains of the middle belt

Cultivation of the land is the major occupation in the middle belt and, as in the north, rotating crops with bush fallow is common. The Tiv, based south east of Makurdi, are one of the main ethnic groups in the region. They begin by clearing the land of its dense bush cover and burn it on the fields before the rains begin. The number of tree stumps and the quantity of roots per unit area is far greater than in the north and clearing the land is extremely hard work. Once cleared, the land is cultivated for four to five years and rotations follow the broad pattern set out below:

Year 1   Yams are usually grown in pure stands as the return on these is good. Demand is particularly high in the forest belt.

Year 2   Sorghum and maize are intercropped, possibly with upland rice for which there is an increasing market.

Year 3   As soil fertility begins to decrease, a rapidly maturing millet is sown to provide food before the main harvest begins which reduces the length of the 'hungry season'. The 'hungry season' is the period towards the end of the crop year when there is little of the previous year's harvest left but the new crop has not been harvested. Alternatively, cash crops of soya or benniseed, for which the Tiv are noted, may be sown but the market for both of these has declined and concentration on food crops is increasing.

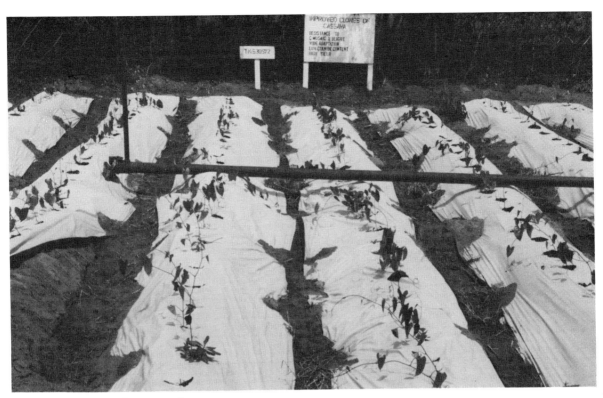
Cultivation of improved varieties of cassava

Year 4 A combination such as sorghum, maize and cassava is grown. The latter is left in the ground well into the fallow. The land has lost much of its fertility by this stage, weeding is becoming a major problem and the tree stumps, cut down and burnt before the first crop, have thrown up suckers and re-established themselves.

After this time, it becomes increasingly difficult, given the limited equipment of the Tiv, to keep the bush at bay. Species such as spear grass (*Imperata cylindrica*) invade and compete with the crops for soil nutrients and light. The land is then usually left to fallow for six to eight years. Research has shown that a high proportion of soil nutrients are restored within this period. Although the nutrient status is lower than if the land had never been cultivated, the soils are still capable of supporting cultivation for several years. This is a further example of how the physical environment influences the farming system. It also shows how local farmers, through trial and error, have developed a system where the fallows are just long enough to allow them to continue farming without destroying the environment.

Overcultivation and declining soil fertility

In spite of conservationist techniques, there has been a gradual decline in soil fertility, as is shown by the replacement of the open forest of the Guinea savanna with grassland in the Tiv region. The change occurs because nutrients are lost at several stages in the cultivation cycle but are never replaced. Each year, when the land is cleared of weeds and the vegetation burnt, nutrients are returned to the soil in the ash but they only become available to crops once the rains begin. Plants can only use a certain quantity of the nutrients and a large proportion is leached out by the rains. The pattern is repeated in subsequent years as the land is burnt prior to cultivation. The amount of ash fertiliser is not as great as in the first year of cultivation after the fallow, and as the plants are still unable to use all the nutrients, loss to the system continues. Careful measures are taken to limit soil erosion: contour ploughing, hoeing, using small fields and intercropping to keep the soil well covered. However, cultivation inevitably leads to losses (see Figure 23, p. 30). Severe gullying in the Tiv region is evidence of this.

Harvesting the crops also removes nutrients from the soil and this adds to its depletion. Organic matter, essential in maintaining the tilth and structure of the soil, declines over the cultivation period. A high humus content guards against erosion and retains nutrients and water.

29

Figure 23   Fertility trends on bush land

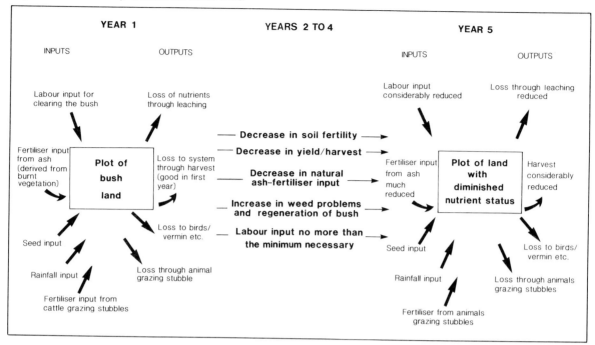

This decline in soil quality is not peculiar to the middle belt but occurs all over Nigeria. Even allowing for population increases, systems such as that of the Tiv would not have degraded the environment had pressure on land not grown because of an increase in demand for cash crops (both food crops within Nigeria and non-food crops for overseas markets).

The overall pattern of rotational bush fallow cultivation is remarkably similar across the plains of the middle belt. In the west of the region, the Nupe, another important ethnic group in the Kontagora region, use similar cropping patterns to the Tiv. Cash crops are important here too, the emphasis being on food crops such as yams, beans, sugar, onions and rice, for Nigerian rather than export markets. Cotton and tobacco are the most important non-food cash crops, the latter being processed at Ilorin. Cultivation is less intensive because of lower population pressures. As a result, more of the forest has survived in the Nupe region. In contrast to the Tiv lands, there is a far higher proportion of *fadama* than of rainfed land and this has enabled the Nupe to concentrate on the production of rice, sugar cane and onions. Forest products are still an important part of the rural economy, in particular the fruits of the locust bean (*Parkia clappertoniana*) and the shea butter tree (*Butyrospermum parkii*), whose fruits yield an edible oil. Contrasts between the Tiv and Nupe agricultural systems are largely due to the differing impact of social and economic variables (see Figure 11, p. 19).

Land use patterns in the highlands of the middle belt

The Jos Plateau rises from the plains to an average height of 1300 m. Undulating, grassy plains are now characteristic of the surface, although these were once covered with vegetation typical of the Guinea savannas with montane characteristics (Figure 22). Intensive cultivation over generations has degraded the soils on the Jos Plateau to the extent that grass is now the dominant cover. The agricultural system differs significantly from the lowland regions. The shortage of land for cultivation has led to a very intensive use of what is available. In a way, patterns are similar to cultivation in the north. According to Morgan (1983), there is an infield-outfield system. On the Plateau the infields are those nearest the homestead. These are intensively cultivated, on an almost continuous basis. This is made possible by heavy use of animal manure (particularly from stall-fed cattle), of composted refuse and of night soil. Crops grown in the composted infields are sorghum, a millet known locally as *acha* (*Digitaria exilis*), peppers, okra, yams, cocoyams, potatoes, sweet potatoes and other temperate vegetables. The intensively cultivated infields are separated from each other by tall hedges.

Intensive cultivation also takes place on the slopes of the Plateau by terracing even the tiniest areas of land. These too are heavily manured and composted. However, in recent years intensive cultivation of the slopes has declined, particularly in the steepest areas.

Plateau farms tend to have their outfields further away from the homestead though still on the Plateau, while farms on or near the slopes may have their outfields on the plains. As Von Thünen's model of agricultural land use suggests, these distant fields are cultivated with crops of less direct importance to the household, frequently cash crops, and the farmer tends to devote less time and organic fertiliser to them. In contrast to the infields, local cattle, as well as those of the visiting Fulani, are turned on to the outfields in the dry season to restore some of the nutrients lost through cultivation.

In the late 1940s there was a significant movement of farmers off the Jos Plateau on to the plains below. The ecology of the new area was quite different and the bush was infested with tsetse fly. The movement was accompanied by the development of the Shendam settlement scheme, a government organised scheme designed to assist the relocation of migrants. In response to the different ecology of the plains, the farmers exchanged the traditional infield-outfield system of the Plateau for the rotational bush fallow system of the plains, where both rainfed and *fadama* lands are cultivated. This illustrates how physical factors influence the nature of the farming system,

and also how adaptable the traditional farmer can be. With little technology available to modify the environment, cropping techniques are modified to get the most out of the land.

Cultivation patterns in the Eastern Highlands do bear some similarities to those on the Jos Plateau. However, in the Adamawa Highlands which follow the border with Cameroon, the soils are poorer than on the Jos Plateau because there is no volcanic parent material. The hills to the north of the Benue River were once forested but have now been degraded to Sudan savanna. South of the Benue the population is extremely sparse. The farmers here terrace the land, use manure, rotate their crops and keep animals. However, the systems have not proved ecologically sound and many farmers have moved on to the lowlands.

The south

The southern Guinea savanna of the middle belt merges into the forested south as the rainfall increases. Rain falls for nine months of the year or more and in the western areas is broken by the 'little dry' in August. This is noticeable to some extent towards the south of

Figure 24   Agricultural land use patterns in the south

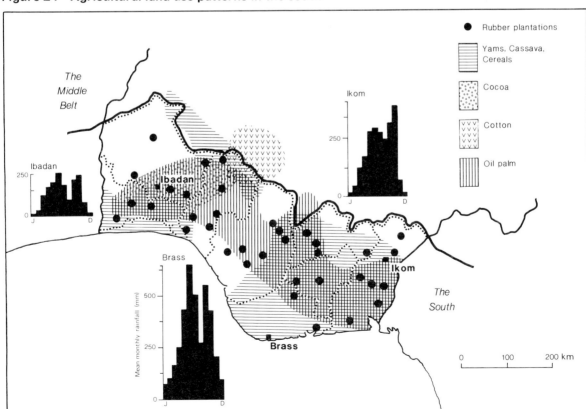

the middle belt but is far more pronounced in the south west. It is barely noticeable in the south east, where rain falls in every month of the year (Figure 24).

Quite what constitutes 'traditional' agriculture presents more of a problem in this southern zone where the indigenous economy was changed beyond recognition by the development of cash, non-food crops by the Europeans. Cocoa dominates the western Yoruba area. Rubber is concentrated in what is now Bendel state. Oil palm is prevalent in the east. As these have been incorporated into farming systems for around a century, they will be considered 'traditional' for the purpose of this book.

The cocoa belt
Three distinct regions emerge in the south, reflecting the cash crop zones (Figure 24). First, the west, the homeland of the Yoruba peoples. This is one of the wealthiest regions of Nigeria because of cocoa farming and commerce. The main cocoa belt extends from Abeokuta for about 320 km and is about 64 km from north to south (Harrison Church, 1980). Abeokuta, Ibadan, Oshogbo, Ondo, Akure, Owo and Ikare are the main centres of the cocoa region. In the centre of this belt, smallholder cocoa cultivation is very intensive, partly due to the fertile loamy soils and the impetus provided by the railway. Thus, in addition to the physical environment, the farmer's decision to grow cocoa is influenced by good access to market.

Throughout West Africa, smallholders combine cash crops with subsistence, so in addition to cocoa, yams, cassava, maize, plantains, citrus fruit, melons, okra, chillies, peppers and tomatoes, a whole range of other crops are produced on domestic farms. The variety of crops cultivated in this zone is far greater than in the north, where savanna soils and limited rainfall put constraints on crop cultivation. It must be stressed that cocoa has traditionally been a smallholder rather than a plantation crop, in contrast with rubber, for example.

Cultivated land usually consists of gardens within the compounds and fields further away from the house. Predictably, the fields nearer the house contain the crops which demand most attention, while those further away require less. The farm thus consists of:

1 a garden with fruit trees and vegetables
2 pure stands of cocoa
3 cocoa under which field crops are grown
4 fields where root crops, cereals and a variety of small crops are intercropped.

The cocoa harvest

Plantation production of plantains

32

Figure 25   The crop year in the south

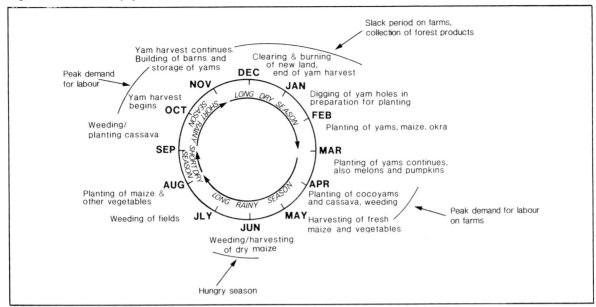

Rotational bush fallow is practised, and, as in the north and the middle belt, the untidy nature of the bush conceals fields in different stages of fallow. The main difference between the bush of the south and that of the middle belt is that fields here tend to be even smaller, weeds and woody species more dense and their regeneration after clearance even more rapid. Keeping the bush at bay is very hard work indeed.

Cocoa cultivation in the central part of the main cocoa belt is so intensive that insufficient subsistence crops are produced. They have to be imported from the south and the north of the cocoa belt where poorer sandy soils and insufficient humidity respectively limit the extent of cocoa. The yam, one of the preferred subsistence crops, is very demanding of soil nutrients. Pressure on land has meant that fallows have been reduced to such an extent that soil nutrient levels do not recover sufficiently to allow the yam to be cultivated. Greater dependence has been placed on supplies of yams from further north in the middle belt, while fruit and vegetables are obtained from the sandy lands to the south of the cocoa belt. Over the years, the area under cassava has increased, an indicator of the growing deterioration in soil quality. Unlike yams, cassava can be grown on the poorest soils.

Cultivation techniques specific to the south
In the northern region farmers can only grow one crop a year, except in the *fadamas*, but in southern Nigeria two crops are possible. As in the rest of the country, the land is cleared before the rains and the vegetation burnt. Mixtures of root crops, bananas and tree crops; maize and small crops; or simply maize and root crops are sown in the ash. These crops do not compete to any great extent for light or nutrients. They are economical in terms of labour and land use, keep soil exposure to a minimum and allow a rotation of crops within the field. Shortly before the end of the 'little dry' in August, an additional crop may be interplanted, replacing one already harvested. This extends the cropping season and effectively, the area cropped (Figure 25). Although this is carried out to a limited extent in the southern Guinea savanna, the harvesting of two crops from rainfed land is really a characteristic of the south.

Farming systems in the rubber zone
To the east of the cocoa belt and in Bendel State in particular, rubber and managed timber reserves are the main non-food cash crops destined for the export market. The soils are sandy, draining rapidly, and heavy rainfall (2285–3050 mm) has left soils severely leached. This is the land of the Bini peoples and the population here is far less dense than in Yorubaland. This is attributable to the effect of slave raiding in the nineteenth century and also to the shortage of water. Ground water is trapped in deep aquifers, so is not easily accessible.

Cropping patterns reveal many similarities with the cocoa belt but rubber replaces cocoa as the chief cash crop (Figure 24). Although rubber does grow wild in

33

this region, unlike cocoa it is primarily an estate rather than a smallholder crop. Some processing takes place on rubber plantations. In this central zone, similar subsistence and food crops for cash tend to be grown by smallholders to those further west, but fallow periods are slightly longer due to lower population pressure. An additional crop in the riverine areas is rice. Warri, Sapele and Benin are the foci for rubber producers and are the major markets of the region where food crops are also traded.

To the north east of the area where communications are still poor, there is heavy concentration on subsistence agriculture. Rice, yams and cotton are the chief crops, together with a wide range of other root crops, cereals and vegetables. Intercropping is common and even the cotton varieties of the south are sufficiently robust to be intercropped. Wherever possible, two crops a year are harvested in order to get as much as possible from a relatively small area.

It is because output is higher, population pressure greater and keeping the bush at bay so much harder, that southern farms tend to be smaller than those in the north — less than three hectares as opposed to around four or five hectares.

Farming systems in the oil palm zone

The oil palm dominates the landscape throughout the south though it is at its most prosperous in the eastern states where it has replaced most of the indigenous rainforest (Figure 24). Here rainfall is very heavy, at least 1780 mm, and although the soils are severely leached the oil palm tolerates the low levels of nutrients and is the main cash crop of the region. In its wild and semi-wild state oil palm is a smallholder crop. However, in recent years, plantation oil palms with far greater production potential have been increasing in importance. Chapter 6 looks specifically at one such plantation scheme.

The agricultural systems of the Ibo whose homelands are in Imo and Anambra States are particularly interesting. Population density among the Ibo is the greatest in Nigeria, frequently exceeding 300 per km², and it is notable that there are few major settlements. The population is dispersed throughout the rural areas. There is a general similarity to cropping patterns further west, the main difference being that oil palm replaces rubber. Typically, farms are organised along the following lines:

1 a garden with fruit trees and vegetables
2 pure stands of oil palm
3 oil palm bush where wild oil palms grow together with some 30 to 40 other species, all of which have marketable produce
4 stands of oil palm beneath which are mixtures of root crops and small crops, okra and peppers, for example
5 fields where root crops, cereals and a variety of small crops are intercropped.

Cultivation is very intensive in Ibo land. With the use of manure, kitchen gardens and fields near the compound are cultivated every year. In the latter, two crops a year are harvested, the second being interplanted among other crop mixtures, thus extending the cultivated area and the growing season. Fields further away from the homestead are involved in typical bush/fallow rotations but the fallow period has been reduced to around three years, quite insufficient for soil recovery. Both women and men cultivate the land, the men usually tending the tree and bush crops while the women concentrate on root crops and vegetables. This contrasts with the Muslim areas of the north where women have little to do with field cultivation.

Summary

Throughout Nigeria traditional farming systems reveal careful adaptation to the environment but at the same time many are examples of ecological systems in decline. This may seem contradictory but increasing population pressure and cash cropping have forced farmers to extract more from the environment than they are returning to it. There are not enough organic or inorganic fertilisers and, anyway, excessive use of the latter can cause further problems. The fallow, the natural system of soil replenishment, has been reduced to a minimum and is frequently not long enough to allow the soil to recover. It is partly in response to this that the ecology of large parts of Nigeria has changed, not least the increase in grassland in formerly forested areas. However, were it not for the ecologically sound techniques of the traditional farmer, the environment would have run downhill more rapidly than it has done. In contrast to many long held views, the farmer is actually a conservationist. This is not to say that traditional farming will of itself provide a solution to Nigeria's need for increased food production. However, there does seem a strong case for combining the best of traditional farming, in particular the sound, underlying ecological principles, with relevant modern technology to extract a great deal more from an environment which is potentially very productive.

Assignments

1 Using Figure 15, describe the types of vegetation found at the following locations:
6°E 5°N   8°E 8°N
6°E 7°N   8°E 11°N

2 Study Figure 14.
(a) Describe and explain the rainfall regime at Kano.
(b) How does the regime differ at Jos? Explain the factors causing the difference.
(c) What accounts for the higher rainfall, and the two rainfall maxima, at Warri?

3 To what extent does the pattern of land use around (i) villages, and (ii) major urban centres, in the northern belt, conform to Von Thünen's theory? What factors, other than distance, influence the pattern?

4 Describe the techniques which make traditional farming in the northern belt 'ecologically conservative'.

5 Construct a flow diagram to show how overcultivation can lead to the problem of declining yields, with particular reference to the middle belt of Nigeria.

6 How does altitude affect farming patterns in Nigeria?

7 Using Figure 11 as a guide, compare and contrast the farming systems of the three main belts in Nigeria.

Questions from A level examination papers

8 Discuss the effects of rainfall amount and seasonality upon agriculture and water supply in West Africa. (Oxford, June 1985)

9 Examine the nature of agriculture and the problems of agricultural development in the 'Middle Belt' of West Africa (Oxford, June 1984)

10 Examine, using examples, the relations between climate and natural vegetation in West Africa. (Oxford, June 1984)

11 With reference to specific examples in Africa:
(a) discuss the physical and human factors that have led to the loss of soil fertility and accelerated soil erosion;
(b) describe and assess the success of the various methods of soil conservation used in different environments and agricultural systems. (Joint Matriculation Board, June 1984)

12 'Rainfall is the principal determinant of the type of agriculture practised in tropical areas'. Critically examine this statement. (London, June 1985)

13 Illustrate the use made of tropical regions characterised by either monsoon climates or savanna climates. (Cambridge, November/December 1985)

14 With reference to one or more countries you have studied, discuss the role of the following in its agricultural geography:
(a) climate and soils;
(b) land tenure and size of holding. (Cambridge, November/December 1984)

4
The Kano River Project: a case study from the north

Nigeria's decision to irrigate

Nigeria's decision to introduce large-scale irrigated farming in the early 1970s was prompted by several factors. Irrigation was ecologically appealing in that (theoretically) it could make dry lands productive and drought a thing of the past. It gave Nigeria a modern image in keeping with its oil economy. It consumed foreign exchange of which there was a surplus by the late 1970s. At the same time it prevented foreign exchange from being spent needlessly on food imports which could be produced at home. Finally, it transferred some of the benefits of oil to the rural sector. The advice of USAID, FAO and the Common-wealth Development Corporation (CDC) helped to convince Nigeria that irrigation could really turn a dream, the end of underdevelopment, into a reality.

The irrigation projects of the north

The first three sites selected for irrigation schemes were in the north:

1 near Kano on the Kano River
2 near Bakolori on the Sokoto River
3 in the southern Lake Chad region.

The projects involved the damming of the Kano and Sokoto rivers to provide a catchment area for the annual floods (Figure 26). Release of water into the river and into irrigation channels on the 20,000 hectares or so of land to be irrigated by each scheme could then be controlled. This produced two distinct areas:

1 the irrigation project land to which water was conducted by canals
2 the floodplain farmland downstream from the irrigation projects.

The South Chad Irrigation Project (SCIP) was different. The lake itself was a reservoir and a deep channel was dug into it to carry the water to the 22,000 hectare irrigation area on its southern shore.

However, irrigation meant more than just a dam and associated 'hardware'. It required project farmers to

'Park farmland' near Kano

Figure 26 Major irrigation projects in northern Nigeria

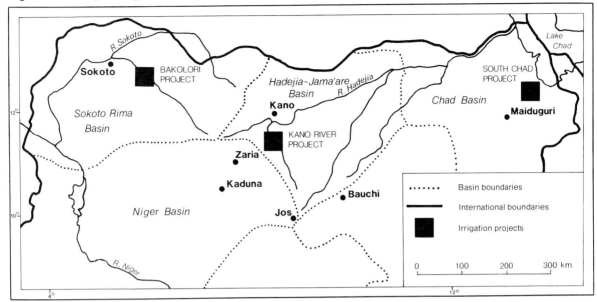

change their approach to farming completely. They were expected to orient themselves towards growing crops for market rather than for subsistence. They had to accept the new concept that cropping need no longer be confined to the six months during which the rains fell. A growing season of 12 months was now possible. Within the project areas farmers could grow vegetables, maize, rice and other cereals during the wet season followed by irrigated wheat in the dry season. Such changes were exciting to the planners but required major physical and mental adjustments by the farmers. As we shall see from the case study of the Kano River Project below, the schemes were rarely as successful as theoretical assumptions would have indicated.

The Kano River Project

Background to the area

In the early 1970s the Kano River Project (KRP) held out high hopes for irrigated agriculture in northern Nigeria. The gently undulating savanna plains around Kano with shallow, light, sandy soils are well-known for their long tradition of permanent as opposed to bush fallow cultivation. Farmers have adapted to the single rainy season and to the minor changes in soil and drainage. As a result, cropping patterns are highly complex, varying according to the local ecology and to the needs of the household. The area is one of the most

densely populated in northern Nigeria (over 550 per km²) and has long supported a dense rural population as well as providing produce for the market at Kano. Local farmers are thus both ecologically and commercially aware.

Traditional farming in the area is essentially of two types, upland and flood plain or *fadama*, the former covering by far the larger area. The early rains fall in April but planting only starts in late May when the rainfall is heavier and more reliable. After reaching a peak in August/September, the rains tail off, ceasing almost entirely by mid-October. Millet and sorghum are the chief staples and are often interplanted with each other. Early millet is harvested in August, while sorghum takes longer and is harvested from late November to early December. Maize has become increasingly popular, mainly because of its short growing period from June to September. It is being encouraged by project officials because of the high national, though not necessarily local, demand. However, maize is far more vulnerable to drought than the traditional cereals of the area.

Each year the Kano, the Sokoto and most of the rivers throughout West Africa flood during the wet season. This is of considerable importance to traditional farming as it is on the seasonally inundated or waterlogged flood plains (*fadamas*) that cultivation is most intensive. *Fadama* soils are highly fertile, their nutrient levels being restored by silt in the annual flood waters. Sugar, rice, vegetables and other minor crops are grown in the areas nearest the rivers. Cultivation continues well into the dry season and as

37

Fulani cattle of the north being taken to pasture

the moisture in the soil dries out, irrigation is possible from shallow wells or directly from the rivers using traditional methods such as the shaduf. Still on the flood plain, though further away from the rivers, sorghum, cotton and groundnuts are common, though irrigation of these is not usual.

Cattle are important in the region. They belong in the main to the semi-nomadic Fulani and are brought into the area around the project for grazing. They tend to be permanent in the region because cultivation is so intensive that grazing land is limited. The cattle consume the crop residues and provide an important source of manure for farms in the area.

The Project

At the heart of the project is the Tiga dam with a reservoir capacity of 20,000 million m³, which is capable of irrigating 70,000 hectares. The target area for irrigation is, however, only 20,000 hectares and is likely to affect no more than 1–2 per cent of the population of Kano State directly. The dam was completed in 1975 but progress was slow and by 1977 only 5000 hectares had actually been irrigated. The scheme has continued to progress as slowly as at the start and there have been numerous problems, mainly due to lack of adequate planning.

The objectives of the Kano River Project (KRP) were much the same as the other large irrigation projects of northern Nigeria:

1 the production of a surplus of wheat and other usually imported crops which would reduce imports and save foreign exchange
2 the improvement of rural living standards by increasing rural productivity.

Fundamental to the scheme was the transport of water from the dam to the project area and with this a transfer of modern irrigation technology to local farmers. A primary canal carried the water from the dam to the project area some 14km away. It was then transported in secondary canals to different blocks of the project area, which ranged from 40 to 240 hectares in area. Distributary canals took water to the individual fields and from there water was fed into the fields. Not every part of each block was irrigated. Some areas were unsuitable as they had bad drainage, for instance. In consequence many farmers had a mixture of irrigated and unirrigated land.

Field level extension workers taught farmers how to make the most of irrigation technology. They were shown the benefits of cropping over a 12 month cycle. They were also instructed in the use of new and improved seed, fertilisers, insecticides and pesticides, as well as other inputs, in the right quantities and at the right time in conjunction with irrigation water. Credit facilities were improved but no formal marketing structure was set up as Kano itself provided a substantial market for local produce. In theory everything was available for the farmer to switch to a more modern and scientific mode of production.

Problems and achievements of the KRP

Hasty planning

Unfortunately, the project's problems still far out-number its benefits. This is not really surprising as irrigated agriculture is very new to the region. The project was put together hastily at a time when Nigeria saw modernisation of traditional farming as the way to increase rural productivity. Neither the country nor the region has a tradition of irrigation, so the expertise needed to plan the projects was limited. This led to a demand for foreigners to establish large-scale irrigation projects and to train middle manage-ment and extension workers. While such foreigners may well have had experience in project design and management elsewhere, the numbers of environmental problems that arose on the KRP reflect the haste with which the project was put together and a lack of understanding of local ecology. Misuse of irrigation water, for example, caused increased salinity problems in the project area.

Shortage of personnel

Although foreigners played a major role in the early management of the project, the bulk of the staff was Nigerian. However, as the project was established so rapidly, many important posts could not be filled for some time because trained personnel were simply not available. Furthermore, working on an irrigation project meant working in the public sector where salaries were lower than in the private sector, particularly in jobs relating to oil. The project thus had problems holding on to the staff it had trained. Field level extension workers, on whom such projects depended, frequently used the project as a stepping stone to better paid employment in the urban areas. Local response to the KPR was often far from enthusiastic. This was mainly because relatively little effort had been devoted to helping farmers understand the changes that were taking place. Some 13,000 farmers had to be relocated to make way for the dam, canals, project buildings and so on. Although compensation was paid, it was at a very low level in most cases. The farmers who were moved were invariably the poorer for the upheaval.

Problems of water delivery

Even the provision of water, so fundamental to the project, proved a problem. The transport of water from the dam to the fields was by a series of canals and the irrigation department was responsible for getting water into the distributaries or field canals. It then became the responsibility of the farmer to open the gates and irrigate his own fields on specific days. In theory this seemed satisfactory but it was not so in practice. The farmer had little control over the flow of irrigation water into the field canals. This was determined by the irrigation staff who had no direct contact with the farmer. The specific needs of the crops being irrigated were therefore not understood. The extension workers should have bridged the gap but this was rarely the case. Because the farmers had little control over the supply of water to the field canals, water was used in a careless fashion. The first farmers to irrigate from the canals on a particular day tended to use too much water or leave the gates open, with the result that the last farmers to irrigate their fields were short of water. This sort of problem seems to be virtually insurmountable.

Maintenance of the field canals has been and still is another point of conflict between farmers and project staff. The situation will not be resolved until there is a better relationship between these two parties, each of whom thinks that the other should be responsible. Meanwhile canal banks continue to collapse and weeds to choke the waterways.

Inadequate testing

Problems arose almost immediately with the newly introduced cropping system. The project aimed to produce traditional crops in the wet season, followed by irrigated wheat and vegetables in the dry season for market, but this posed problems. Wet and dry season crops conflicted with, rather than complemented, each other. Wheat has to be sown by mid-November. Early millet, a traditional wet season crop, can be harvested in August/September but sorghum is only ready by mid-November, which leaves no time at all for land preparation for wheat. The alternative was for farmers to combine wheat in the dry season with maize in the wet season, as maize has a much shorter growing season, from June to September. The demand for maize in the urban areas was reflected by substantial imports and, as with wheat, all efforts were being made to increase domestic production. Local opinion, however, differed. Maize was an unpopular choice as the dominant wet season crop. It was not a popular source of food locally, nor was it as nutritious as sorghum. Rather than give up cultivating sorghum, many farmers preferred to forgo their wheat crop, which went against the objectives of the project. If they grew wheat and maize at the expense of subsistence crops, it meant having to buy food. Not only was this an alien practice for the traditional farmer but it was costly, particularly in the late 1970s and early 1980s when inflation was high.

Weak management

While the project appeared to provide all that the farmer should need, this was not the case. Irrigated land was ploughed and levelled in the first year of the project. It then became the responsibility of the farmers to prepare their own land. Although there was no training service, farmers were encouraged to use a tractor with or without the know-how, and many did so. Land preparation was invariably a rushed job, crammed into a few weeks. Who had access to the tractor first became an important issue in local politics. In addition, delays were inevitable. Farmers had insufficient funds to pay for tractor hire in advance, or if they had, fuel ran out or machinery broke down and there were too few mechanics to cope with the demand. Similarly, seed, fertiliser, insecticide and pesticide were all provided by the project but owing to administrative hiccoughs supplies often arrived too late or were insufficient to meet the farmers' needs. Inputs had to be paid for in advance and farmers had to borrow heavily to do this. Although many traditional farmers were accustomed to borrowing, the levels of debt caused by the project were far greater than most farmers had anticipated.

Labour shortage, particularly at peak periods, proved to be a further problem. Project organisers overestimated the farmers' access to family labour. Labour costs were yet another financial burden on the farmer.

Unequal benefits

It is easy to list the problems of the Kano River Project. While many of these were no more than teething problems, some fundamental difficulties nonetheless existed. Some of the crop combinations proved inappropriate. Salinity of the soil was sometimes brought about by irrigation, lowering productivity. In some areas crop output was lowered by attacks from pests such as nematode worms. As a result of these problems much irrigable land has remained under-used. Furthermore, inequalities in landholdings have reduced the effectiveness of the project. Larger farmers tend to have more resources to buy fertiliser and seed in advance and to pay for land preparation. They can also grow both project crops and their own food, simply because they have sufficient land to do so. The smaller farmer frequently has not got enough land to do this and so has to choose between commercial and subsistence production. Having lost money from low-yielding project crops, from expensive inputs and from having to buy food to eat, many smaller farmers have abandoned the project crops and have continued growing traditional crops on irrigated project land. This has contributed to the low output from the project area and to an increased difference in income between large and small farmers.

It is more difficult to chronicle the achievements of the KRP. Some farmers have reaped the benefit from

sales of tomatoes and fresh vegetables grown in the dry season, which was impossible before the advent of irrigation. Apart from this, however, direct benefits have been relatively few.

Realistically, one might expect problems in a project of this scale given the rate at which it was established and the limited expertise available. However, the introduction of irrigation can be viewed as an achievement in itself. As local expertise in the use of irrigation water is developed, as indeed it will be, the project is likely to reveal some positive benefits for local producers.

Other irrigation projects

While this case study has focussed mainly on Kano, the situation in the other projects, the Bakolori and the South Chad Irrigation Project (SCIP), was remarkably similar (although the SCIP did not involve a dam). The problems were similar too, and in the Bakolori project resentment by local people of the changes imposed on them was far greater than at Kano. In the SCIP, irrigated farming declined soon after the project started as lake levels fell so low that irrigation was virtually impossible. All in all, the projects have not been successful so far. The vast financial investment in them has been far from justified by the returns. According to Andrae and Beckman (1985), wheat was being imported into Nigeria in the early 1980s at around $150 per tonne and being produced in the north at around $800 per tonne. The initial government subsidy had to be large but it has continued to be very costly. To date, therefore, home grown wheat is far from being an economically viable substitute for the imported product. Similarly, rice production in the Sokoto region has proved to be so expensive that the crop cannot compete in price with imported rice.

Downstream effects of the dam

As they control river flood levels, the Tiga and Bakolori dams affect not only their respective irrigation project areas but also conditions on the flood plains downstream. The dams have brought disadvantages to farmers cultivating the downstream *fadamas* of the Sokoto and Kano Rivers. Controlled flooding has reduced the extent of wet season flooding in the *fadamas*, the depth to which the land is inundated, and the duration of the flood. This has caused changes in both wet and dry season cropping, the most significant being a fall in the production of rice — the very crop that the dams were intended to increase. In the Sokoto valley, Adams (1985) has noted an increase in the cultivation of dry land crops such as millet and sorghum on lands that were once the drier *fadamas*. Farmers are thus having to grow crops which are less rewarding financially.

The fall in rice production, the problems faced by farmers on the irrigation project areas and the chaos in the downstream *fadamas* have all made the dams far less attractive economically than was indicated by the original feasibility studies. Clearly the disadvantages have outweighed any advantages that might have accrued and much skill and trained manpower will have to be invested to correct the errors.

Summary

The Kano River Project undoubtedly has potential. One of the greatest causes of trouble was that it was ill thought out and hastily established. Some of the problems that the KRP and other large-scale irrigation schemes in the north have created will be difficult to reverse. The environment has suffered, especially where salinity problems have been severe.

Treatment of the human population has been callous to say the least. The farmer, who should have been the pivot of the scheme, has been virtually disregarded and was considered ignorant, uneducated and in much need of 'modernisation'. The one-way flow of information from project officials to farmers reflects this disregard for the farmers' expertise and the belief that they could contribute little to the establishment of a modern farming system. Farmers have been kept ill-informed of the changes being made in their areas. With very little warning some 13,000 cultivators were displaced to accommodate project infrastructure. As the modernisation programme has left many poorer than before, it is not surprising that there is widespread disenchantment with the scheme. At the start of the project the small proportion of the state's farmers who would benefit from irrigation were envied. There is now widespread relief that disruption was confined to so few.

In spite of the many problems, these three original large-scale irrigation projects were extended and River Basin Development Authorities (RBDAs) were established in every state with the exception of Lagos State. Between 1983 and 1985, the RBDAs' responsibilities were extended to incorporate rural development and they became the River Basin and Rural Development Authorities (RBRDAs). Since President Babangida came to power in 1985, their responsibilities have been reduced, so that they can concentrate on providing irrigation water in the right quantity, in the right place and at the right time. So far there has been no marked improvement in the performance of these projects.

Assignments

Questions from A level examination papers

1 'Modern agricultural techniques have introduced as many problems as they have solved'. Discuss, giving examples. (London, January 1983)

5

The Lafia Agricultural Development Project: a case study from the middle belt

The Lafia Project, situated in south central Plateau State (Figure 27) is one of Nigeria's Agricultural Development Projects (ADPs). Masterminded by the World Bank, ADPs have focussed on improving traditional agriculture, unlike the irrigation projects of the north which introduced completely new technology to the farmer. The original ADPs were in the north, centred on Funtua, Gusau and Gombe. Although these had their fair share of problems, they offered some hope for improving agricultural productivity and have been extended to other parts of Nigeria. Even now, when government support for most agricultural development schemes has been withdrawn, the ADPs continue to receive government funding, a testimony to their value in the rural areas.

The two basic objectives of the ADPs

1 An increase in agricultural production by improving traditional farming. This was to be achieved by intensive extension work and by the use of inputs such as improved seed, fertilisers, insecticides and pesticides.
2 Development of a local infrastructure, in particular an improved and extended road network, improved services and credit facilities. These enable farmers to obtain essential inputs as and when they need them and provide a marketing structure for easy sale of agricultural surpluses.

On the completion of many rural development schemes, the project farmer is left high and dry — short of essential inputs, unable to obtain fuel or spare parts for his machinery and lacking the expertise to repair machinery when it breaks down. The system based on modern technology is thus brought to a halt. The ADPs aimed to avoid such chaos. Investment in local infrastructure and services was an important part of the projects as was information for the farmer. What has made the ADPs particularly appealing is

that they have caused little physical disruption. Farmers have not had to be relocated. What is more, farmers remain the main decision-makers on their farms, at liberty to accept or reject the advice of project officials. At the same time, few would dispute that infrastructural developments, in particular the improved road network, now benefit entire communities in most ADP zones.

Background to the Lafia Project

The Lafia Project conformed to the basic pattern of the ADPs in that its aims were, and still are, to increase the agricultural output of the region's small farmers by improving traditional cultivation.

Covering an area of around 9400 square kilometres, the Project is in the Guinea savanna zone and receives on average around 1200 mm of rain a year, spread over seven to eight months. Ecologically it is in the transitional zone between the drier Sudan savanna lands of the north and the forested south. As one

Traditional farming on the Jos Plateau

Figure 27 Lafia Agricultural Development Project

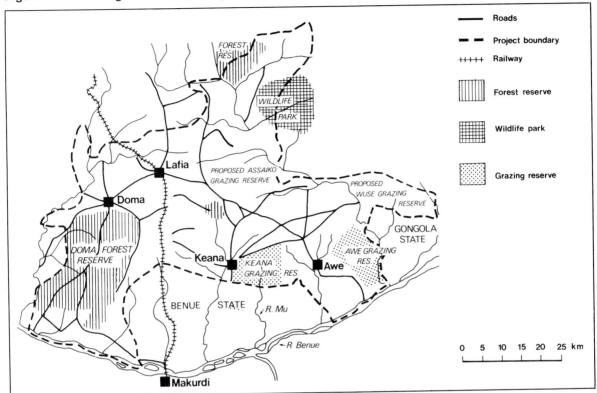

would expect, the scenery consists of grassy savanna with patches of forest. On the farms, grains typical of the northern economy are grown alongside root crops from the south. Mixed farming is the norm for the region with some two-thirds of the area being intercropped. Sorghum is the chief crop and is grown on two-thirds of the land. It is usually combined with other cereals such as maize and millet or with root crops such as yams and cassava. Sometimes three crops are grown in the same field, sorghum, maize

and yams being a popular combination. The aim is not only to get the most out of the soil but also to limit land preparation and maintenance in a region where bush and weeds regenerate rapidly and where population pressure on land is high.

Crop combinations are numerous and vary according to the local ecology and to the preferences of the numerous ethnic groups in the region. The Tiv, the

Sorghum ready for harvest

Figure 28 Major ethnic groups in the Lafia ADP area

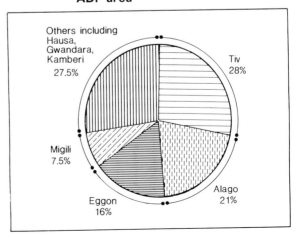

43

Alago and the Eggon together constitute some 65 per cent of the population (Figure 28) but overall there are around 30 different ethnic groups living in the project area. Social and economic organisation varies enormously in these groups but on average the cultivated area is around three hectares per household. When the project was first established, the rural population was estimated at 52,070 families. However, the popularity of the scheme has drawn people to the area and the number of rural inhabitants is now believed to be much higher.

Major elements of the Lafia ADP

The Lafia Project was inaugurated in 1977. The implementation phase continued until 1982/83, during which time the major elements of the scheme were established. These are shown in Table 7, the core of the scheme being in heavy type. Infrastructure and services development includes the construction of roads and essential buildings for the project and the establishment of specific services to help the project function properly. Such services include:

1 staffing, in particular the training of extension workers
2 the provision of credit
3 the provision of a marketing structure.

On the agricultural side (Table 7), the extension of information to farmers concentrated on such issues as:

1 how and when to apply a range of inputs such as fertilisers, insecticides and pesticides
2 the benefits of mechanisation where appropriate.

The scheme has tried to give farmers new information and also the scope to use these innovations in the long term.

In addition to the core elements, a livestock programme, which included fisheries and poultry development; forestry; large farm schemes and a rice scheme have been incorporated into the Project (Table 7). These have put an enormous strain on the Lafia ADP and as a result most have not been successful.

The Lafia ADP's achievements

Lafia ADP achieved some notable results. There was an overall increase in crop yield, particularly attributable to yam cultivation. The road network improved dramatically. There was an increased awareness of modern farming techniques, an improvement in input supplies, and an increase in the number of wells. All these improvements have directly benefited the rural population.

Improvements to the road network were particularly

impressive. The target was to reconstruct and improve 280 km of local government roads and to upgrade an additional 320 km of community-built tracks to the same standard. By the end of the project 804 km of new road had been built, thereby exceeding initial targets by 34 per cent. Substantial benefits resulted from the extended road network. Surveys showed an increase in the level of four-wheeled vehicle traffic and in the movement of passengers and goods in the Project area. New feeder roads helped to reduce the gap between urban and rural commodity prices. In one area for example, yam prices were only 45 per cent of Lafia town prices before the construction of a Project feeder road. In the following year, when the feeder road had been completed, yam prices rose to 70 per cent of Lafia town levels. In subsequent years they reached 90 per cent. Surveys revealed that over the five years of the Project, the additional revenue from marketed crops in areas served by roads more than equalled the cost of their construction.

However, roads need maintenance and so far this has been limited. One of the Project's aims was that maintenance should be shared by the Project and the local government councils at first but would gradually be taken over by the latter. Sadly, maintenance of the road network has been minimal and is a problem that still needs to be tackled.

Finally, as a result of the Project, a more highly trained group of people, with at least some experience of how to run such a scheme, exists in the ADP zone.

Problems and pitfalls of the Lafia ADP

Funding and cashflow

The Lafia ADP's funding was shared between the World Bank, the Federal Government of Nigeria and the Plateau State Government (Table 8). Lafia was unique among the ADPs at that time in that the state government provided the largest portion of the funds in both absolute and relative terms. Throughout the implementation phase total project funding reached 91 per cent of the levels expected. However, the timing of payment was so erratic as to cause major cashflow problems. To understand why the Project's progress was brought to an abrupt halt in year 5, it is necessary to examine the timing of payments.

Year 1 In year 1, funding from all sources was far below what was expected. This hindered the housing and wells programmes among others. During most of year 1, the Lafia ADP's cashflow problems were severe, as over half the payments were received only in the final quarter. Even before it had got under way, the project had difficulty meeting bills and paying salaries. This did little to boost the morale of employees.

Year 2 State funding improved in the second year but in spite of this, cumulative funding from the federal government and from the World Bank remained at less than 50 per cent of what had been expected by the ADP.

Year 3 By the third year, funding was far better organised and closer to the expected levels. For the first time the Lafia ADP really started to move forward.

Years 4 and 5 In the final two years problems surfaced again. Between 1981 and 1983, state and federal government funding was often very late and was not even sufficient to cover the costs of recurrent expenditure, let alone finance new developments.

Table 7   Major components of the Lafia ADP

Development of rural infrastructure	Development of services	Agricultural development
Civil works including **improvement and extension of road network**	**Staffing/management training**	**Improvement of small (2–3 ha) farms' crop production levels through extension work,** including the use of modern technology, improved seed/fertiliser/ herbicides, machinery (where available and appropriate)
Project building, e.g. housing for staff, workshops, offices, services	**Establishment of demonstration units**	
Improvement of rural water supply	**Record keeping**	**Seed multiplication programme**
	Provision of credit	Improvement of larger farm crop production levels
	Assistance with marketing	Establishment of large farms through group farming
	Farm management and advisory service (mainly geared towards capital intensive farming)	Promotion of modern technology, including capital intensive methods
		Federal large-scale rice production
		Livestock, including poultry and fisheries development
		Forestry

Note: Core features of programme appear in heavy type. Many projects were 'added on' in the early stages of the programme or, in the case of the rice scheme, appended with little planning much later.

Table 8   Sources of funding for the Lafia ADP

Sources of funds	Estimated (million naira)	Actual (million naira)	Percentage of estimate
Plateau State	22.3	19.0	85
Federal Government	12.1	9.6	79
World Bank	15.9	14.8	93
Additional	—	2.4	
Total	50.3	45.8	91

World Bank funds had to be directed away from development activities to fill the gap and project expansion was brought to a halt in year 5, when recurrent expenditure absorbed all available funds. 356 project staff and 1000 casual labourers were laid off, 70 per cent of project vehicles were withdrawn from daily use and were physically locked into compounds so that they were unavailable. Essential extension work was halted and cash loans promised to farmers under the credit scheme were cancelled. Payment of local salaries and wages was delayed and by 1983 (the sixth year of the Project's life), salaries were being paid one or two months in arrears. Morale on the Project was low, farmers were losing interest. The original aim of extension workers continuing to take new ideas to farmers had floundered and in general the operation seemed to be going wrong.

Agricultural development

Much more could have been achieved at farm level The agricultural side of the Lafia ADP was never as successful as the infrastructural and services side. One of the reasons for this was that successive project managers found it easier to deal with objects such as roads and buildings, rather than people. Ironically, a scheme which set out to improve the traditional farming system revealed that it had failed to understand the reasoning behind many traditional farming practices.

Before the establishment of the Lafia ADP and in its very earliest stages, state agricultural officials evaluated traditional farming in the area and put forward production targets. Rather than suggesting improvements to the existing mixed cropping system, it was proposed that monocropping should be substituted, a system which would have actually reduced small farm output. Misunderstanding of the traditional systems due to inadequate field experience can be the only explanation for this misjudgement. To show how serious it was, Bivins, in the Project Completion Report (Department of Rural Development, 1984) cites examples of mistaken yield estimates made by agricultural experts before the Project started. Surveys conducted during the ADP showed that yields under traditional mixed farming had been seriously under-estimated. In some cases, yield projection levels were already being achieved under the traditional cropping system (Table 9). Thus what was being proposed was of little benefit to local traditional farmers. Fortunately, Project farmers were more discerning than Project officials in their choice of techniques.

The extension services were ill equipped to advise Investment in the extension services was pitifully small in view of their fundamental role. The aim of the Project was to train sufficient field level extension workers to make the extension worker/ farmer ratio 1:500. This was easily achieved but although field level workers were available in quantity, the quality of their training frequently fell below acceptable limits. The reasons are clear. Towards the end of the 1970s and even in the early 1980s people from the rural areas were still flocking to the towns in search of a better standard of living. In addition, education and the media encouraged the belief that the rural life was something 'left behind' by the developed nations. In consequence, few wanted to devote their lives to working in rural areas. In spite of this, it was not difficult to recruit large numbers of potential field extension workers as jobs in the cities were short and alternative opportunities were few. Many simply accepted the training as a stop gap until something better, and preferably urban-based, turned up. There was thus a shortage of the right sort of field level extension workers. Those recruited often had a limited background in agriculture and little enthusiasm to see the Project succeed. This attitude, coupled with the dissemination of information which was not

Table 9   Misjudgement of the potential of the traditional farming system by agricultural officers in the Lafia ADP

	Pre-project estimates of yield under traditional farming systems in project area	Predicted improved yield under monocropping	Actual total crop yield from traditional crop mixtures (1981–82)
Sorghum	600 kg/ha	1200 kg/ha	Sorghum/millet mixture 1565 kg/ha
Maize	600–750 kg/ha	1750 kg/ha	Sorghum/maize 1769 kg/ha
Yams	6 t/ha	10–15 t/ha	10 t/ha

Table 10 Estimated and actual fertiliser sales in the Lafia ADP

	Apr 1978– Mar 1979	Apr 1979– Mar 1980	Apr– Dec 1980	Jan– Dec 1981	Jan– Dec 1982
Pre-Project estimates of likely fertiliser sales in the Project area (tonnes)	1726	3765	6271	9501	13,693
Total sales (tonnes)	2313	3580	5495	6605	12,063
Percentage of estimate	134	95.08	87.63	69.52	88.10

always of benefit or relevant to the farmer, reduced the chances of extension workers succeeding with their objectives at village level.

Throughout Africa, rural workers do not receive much respect, so the field level extension workers felt that their jobs brought little prestige. They were despised by the 'pen pushers' who, although conceding that they were essential to the Project, preferred not to liaise with field level workers. The farmer, too, was a despised member of society because of his 'ignorance' and lack of formal education. No value was put on his ability to produce crops. Partly because of such attitudes, partly because of the quality of field level workers and partly because of the shortage of senior personnel in crucial posts, the extension system has not enjoyed its anticipated success.

In spite of their many shortcomings, the extension services have had *some* positive results. Of the recommended inputs, fertiliser adoption was relatively good in the Lafia Project and would have been better had supplies to the Project not been delayed. Sales rose from 2313 tonnes at the commencement of the Project to 12,063 tonnes in year 5 (Table 10). Improvements in the use of other inputs was not as dramatic. Next to fertiliser, improved seed and yam set dressing were the inputs most in demand. There was growing interest in improved seed varieties but use of insecticides and pesticides was low. The lack of extension work to promote these products may have led to a lack of awareness of their potential benefit among farmers.

Problems caused by the Project being too diffuse

It is arguable that, had the Project been smaller, more compact and focussed directly on the core elements, its achievements would have been greater. The peripheral projects were numerous and stretched the already limited resources of the Lafia ADP. They included a livestock scheme which involved grazing reserves and animal health development; poultry breeding; fisheries in bunded lagoons; and forestry projects for the generation of firewood. Although it was a prime aim of the ADPs to reach the small farmer, the Lafia Project also approached larger farm units with attempts at community farming and a large-scale rice production project. The low rates of economic return for the Lafia ADP as a whole have been largely attributed to the failure of many of these peripheral schemes to produce the expected returns. Overall planning was poor. Two peripheral projects illustrate this clearly.

Farm group projects Originally there were few large farms in the Project area. In an attempt to achieve the economies of scale possible on large farms, several farmers were encouraged to farm together on areas ranging from 5 to 75 hectares. These groups were assigned an extension agent to advise, supervise and assist with the record keeping. One group even received a tractor loan. However, success was limited. Farmers invariably proved more interested in farming their own rather than the communal fields. Loans not repaid and expenditure not recovered from these farm groups contributed to the poor economic performance of the Lafia ADP.

The rice project In 1981, in response to a government directive to all ADPs to increase their rice production, Lafia rapidly launched the Federal Rice Production Programme. 1786 hectares were cleared, extension workers were assigned to the scheme and inputs of seed, fertiliser and herbicides were obtained, as was credit for rice production. The speed at which the scheme was assembled was quite remarkable and it could have been successful. However, once again management problems emerged and caused chaos on the agricultural side. Initially, extension workers focussed on training small farmers in the techniques of rice production. The emphasis soon shifted to direct production on two large blocks of land in the alluvial flood plains at Jangwa and Rukubi. Blocks of some 50 hectares each were assigned to groups of farmers. While a few did well, the internal organisation of others was poor and resulted in a complete failure.

Throughout the project there was always a tendency for farmers to give more time to their own fields than to the rice. Serious problems with weeds occurred, land preparation was not of the highest quality, and at harvest time late arrival of the combines contributed to heavy losses. At Rukubi, weed seed was so intermixed with rice that the Nigerian Grains Board refused to purchase the crop and it had to be sold locally at some 70 per cent of the Grains Board price. Insufficient mechanical equipment had been supplied by the federal government. Machinery had to be diverted to the rice project from other programmes on the ADP, particularly from the much needed road development and maintenance work, and from the forestry and livestock programmes which were already well behind schedule. The small farmer extension programme was disrupted as officials were transferred to the rice scheme and other activities were cut to provide funds for the new programme. Potential for producing rice does exist but undertaking such a scheme at such speed was inevitably disastrous. The rice project directly affected the rest of the ADP as it meant that the Project's resources were spread more thinly.

Summary

The problems associated with the Project were largely managerial. Given time and a more experienced managerial staff, most of the Lafia ADP's problems could be rectified.

The Project's main achievements were due to the farmers' freedom to select what would benefit them most from the recommendations made by trained (but nonetheless agriculturally inexperienced) extension workers. The most striking example is the increase in yam production. The extension services virtually ignored yam production, which was another error in the Project's assessment of local agriculture. The yam was the farmer's most profitable crop. It is notable that the heaviest use of fertilisers was for yams and improved seed and yam set dressing was the next most popular input. Thus the farmer was discerning and selected the input or method which offered most potential for increased production. This reflects the value of an integrated agricultural development project. Although the scheme centres on the spread of information and inputs to farmers, it nonetheless allows the farmer the freedom to accept or reject project recommendations. Had the farmer not been able to use any of his skill and judgement, the overall increase in Lafia's output would have been less than it was in the first five years. The increased output was largely due to an increase in yam rather than cereal production. It was not really based on methods recommended by the extension services.

It was not realistic to expect the Lafia ADP to work after only a few years. The experience of the Project was new for both farmers and Nigerian project managers and it will take time for things to settle down. As the majority of the Project's shortcomings were managerial rather than environmental, there is plenty of opportunity for improvement. Even in the first five years, there were some positive achievements.

Assignments

Questions from A level examination papers

1 Discuss, with reference to one or more case studies from developing countries, the problems involved in the transition from subsistence to commercial agriculture. (Cambridge, November/ December 1984)

2 Consider, with detailed examples, some of the problems involved in attempts to modernise agriculture in developing countries. (Oxford and Cambridge, July 1981)

6
Palm oil production: Risonpalm, a case study from the south

The oil palm is indigenous to West Africa and is among the most valuable of the tree crops in southern Nigeria. Palm leaves are used for thatching, the ribs in building and the fibre for making rope. The tree is tapped for palm wine, although this weakens it considerably, and the clusters of fruit yield the characteristic red palm oil. Nigerians have always valued palm oil and traditionally it has proved a highly nutritious part of the local diet. The Europeans also appreciated its potential and, by the early 20th century, Nigerian smallholders were selling their palm products. In particular, palm oil was exported to Britain. Here it provided oil which maintained machinery for Britain's developing industries. It also became an important raw material for the manufacture of cooking oil, margarine, soap, candles and a vast range of other products, including paints. A means of extracting oil from palm kernels was also devised in Britain and these too were exported from Nigeria. Figure 29 shows the astronomic rise in Nigeria's palm oil exports to Britain. By 1900, Nigeria supplied the bulk of world demand for palm oil but by 1938 her position as the world's leading supplier had been surpassed by Indonesia and Malaysia. Here production was entirely from plantation palms, the yield and quality of which were far higher than from the wild and semi-wild West African palms.

In this chapter we shall restrict our interest to palm oil as this, of all the products from the oil palm, is of major economic importance to Nigeria.

The oil palm, ecological requirements

High temperatures and rainfall, the chief requirements of the oil palm, limit it to southern Nigeria and the southern coast of West Africa (see Figure 30, p. 50). The oil palm likes sunlight, so tends not to be found in the high forest. Where the forest has been

Figure 29   Palm oil exports from Nigeria

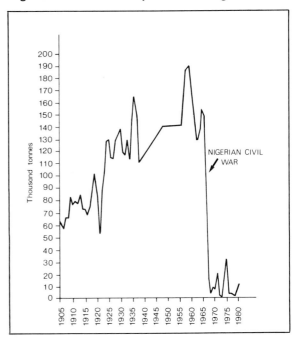

cleared for human habitation, stands of oil palm are at their most dense. They grow wild and seedlings from the wild plants are planted near villages and homesteads by the local people. Neither the wild nor the semi-wild transplanted palms are given much attention until they start bearing, when their fruit is harvested. Cultivated oil palm is increasingly being grown on plantations.

If sunlight is available, the palm thrives where annual rainfall is around 2000 mm, spread over at least eight months of the year. South eastern Nigeria is thus its preferred habitat, although it dominates the landscape throughout southern Nigeria. The palm can tolerate

Figure 30   Main oil palm areas of West Africa

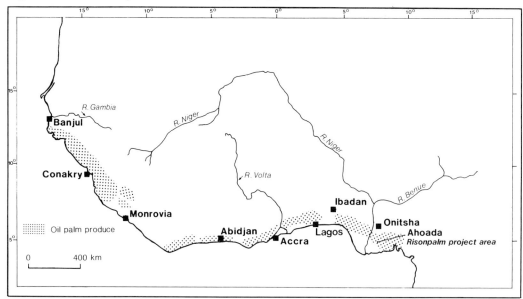

as little as 1300 mm of rainfall, though this has to be well distributed throughout the year. What really limits its northerly extent is the distinct dry season. Oil palm can and does grow on the sandy soils which are not suitable for cocoa but its yield increases greatly in deep, well drained loams with plentiful nutrients.

In the wild and semi-wild state palms grow to over 12 m, rising above the secondary forest into the direct sunlight. They only begin bearing fruit from about their tenth year. By comparison, the cultivated palm is much shorter, around 6 m high, and starts bearing at around six years or even earlier. The clusters of fruit on the cultivated palms are more numerous and heavier than on the wild palms. The fruit is of better quality and easier to harvest. Clusters of palm fruit on plantation trees are harvested from the ground by means of a knife at the end of a long pole but oil palm harvesting in the wild is a more risky and skilful business, as the trees have to be climbed before the bunches of fruit can be cut.

Extracting the oil

The palm fruit (Figure 31) has a kernel at its centre which is surrounded by a hard shell, a fibrous mesocarp and a tough, leathery skin or pericarp. It is the fibrous mesocarp and the kernel which yield the oil. The wild palm fruit in West Africa has a relatively thin mesocarp compared with plantation fruit and its South East Asian rivals. In consequence, the oil yield from wild and semi-wild palms is relatively low. Extracting the oil is no easy task. Two traditional methods are still used in West Africa:

The 'hard oil' process Once cut, the clusters of fruit are left to ferment. They are then trampled by foot, boiling water is poured over them and the oil skimmed off the surface. The 'hard oil' process is so-called because the oil melts at a higher temperature than in the 'soft oil' process outlined below. It is quicker than the 'soft oil' process, though the oil contains a higher proportion of undesirable free fatty acids. Some 65 per cent of the available oil in the mesocarp is extracted by the 'hard oil' process. The palm nuts remain intact and, after the oil has been removed, the women crack them open and sell the kernels.

The 'soft oil' process This is a much lengthier process during which the palm fruit is boiled, pounded, reheated and the oil skimmed off. The process yields

Figure 31   The interior of the palm fruit

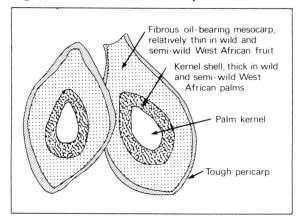

Fibrous oil-bearing mesocarp, relatively thin in wild and semi-wild West African fruit

Kernel shell, thick in wild and semi-wild West African palms

Palm kernel

Tough pericarp

50

only 55 per cent of the total oil available in the mesocarp. The oil melts at a lower temperature than in the 'hard oil' process. The free fatty acid content is low, and the quality of the oil is better. This is because fresh rather than fermented fruit can be used. Soft oil is an important ingredient in a wide range of products, including margarine, soap with a high glycerine content and toiletries.

Efforts to improve Nigerian palm oil production

By the beginning of the twentieth century, research had revealed that oil palms in plantations were more productive than wild and semi-wild stock. However, plantation agriculture was forbidden in British colonies and when in 1907 William Hesketh Lever made the first of several attempts to establish oil palm plantations in Nigeria as a raw material supply for the European soap industry, he was prevented from doing so. Although smallholder production was lower in efficiency, the Nigerian colonial government was adamant that the agricultural resources of the West African colonies should be developed by the indigenous population and that no foreigner should be allowed to own the freehold of the land. Palm oil thus remained the concern of the smallholder until independence. Since then, oil palm plantations have increased and now have such features as on-site processing facilities and labour lines (housing for the labour force).

The colonial administration was not averse to increasing palm oil production and a two-pronged approach was introduced, mainly to assist small-holders, the chief producers of palm oil. On the agricultural side, efforts were concentrated on distributing seedlings of improved quality which would produce fruit with a higher oil content than the indigenous varieties. This was relatively unsuccessful because it was difficult to spread information to the widely-dispersed producers. While many farmers who did hear of the improved stock were eager to try it, the fear that they would ultimately be taxed by the colonial administration for planting improved trees was a disincentive.

In contrast, technical innovations, particularly in methods of oil extraction, were much more successful and the introduction of small-scale oil presses transformed the oil production process for many smallholders. The new presses cost more than £17 in the mid-1930s, which is estimated to be £3 more than the annual income of an oil palm farmer. Also, they were first introduced at the height of the inter-war depression. Despite these facts, there were over 650 presses in use in eastern Nigeria in 1938. With government assistance, thousands more farmers were converted to the use of machinery during the late 1940s.

Problems facing the Nigerian palm oil industry

The good fortune of the smallholder did not last. From the mid-1950s, the Nigerian government turned to larger scale production of palm oil. High levies on palm produce were introduced, crippling the small-holder, and development of the Pioneer Oil Mill which was suitable for large-scale processing of West African palm fruit contributed further to a sharp reduction of the smallholders' profit margin. This situation persisted throughout the 1960s. Although the smallholder was hard hit, large-scale production of palm produce was far from the success that the government had hoped for. Managerial inefficiency, plantations plagued by pests and disease and the civil war (1967–70) caused commercial palm oil production to decline. Since the early 1970s, the government, assisted by the World Bank, has been encouraging the

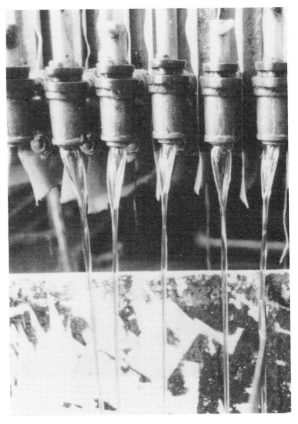

A palm oil factory

distribution of improved quality oil palms to the smallholder in an attempt to boost the joint production of palm produce and food. Once again, attempts have met with limited success as many farmers are wary and many have moved out of farming as a result of the oil boom. The decline in domestic palm oil production, coupled with an increased demand for palm products in Nigeria (the result of a growing population and a rise in demand from both the domestic consumer and industry), has resulted in the country becoming a substantial importer of palm oil. It is in an effort to reverse this trend that agricultural projects have been introduced to raise domestic palm oil production. Risonpalm in Rivers State is one such case.

The Risonpalm Project

Concern over the decline in palm oil production was not as great as it would have been had Nigeria not been enjoying a boom based on its petroleum wealth. However, some projects to rehabilitate the agricultural sector were set in motion and the World Bank was heavily involved in many of these from the early 1970s. Risonpalm in Rivers State was one such oil palm development scheme in which the World Bank has played a substantial part. The Project is entirely owned by the state government but the World Bank has funded 36 per cent of the total cost of 54 million naira. The state and federal governments together have provided most of the remaining funds. Because of its sizeable financial input, the World Bank has had a major say in the operation.

First, the Bank required that the scheme be heavily oriented towards the smallholder. In spite of some resistance to this, Risonpalm has largely complied with this demand. The project consists of a core plantation of 10,000 hectares at Abima. A further 10,000 hectares of smallholder oil palm plantation at Ahoada (see Figure 30, p. 50) is being added to this core. One purpose of the core plantation was to increase domestic palm production. However, it was also hoped that it would create an awareness among smallholders of the value of modern techniques such as improved quality palms, the use of fertiliser and, where necessary, pesticides. For the scheme to function efficiently, an extensive infrastructure was required, including an improved road network, particularly for transporting produce to market; a range of buildings to house and train project staff; offices; stores; and mills for extracting the oil from both fruit and kernels. A market for the final product was already available through the marketing board.

Oil palm nursery on the Risonpalm plantation

The second factor with which Rivers State had to comply before World Bank funding was made available, was that the project should be operated, at least in its early stages, by foreign project managers. Risonpalm had to agree to this and a Belgian company, Socfin Consultancy Services (Socfinco) was assigned to the task. This meant that key positions in the Project were held by foreign personnel. It was they who would train Nigerians to take over senior management positions in due course. The Belgians' expertise in project management outside their home country was considerable but, unfortunately, Socfinco personnel were no experts in oil palm production. Furthermore, Socfinco officials were in charge of establishing the Project, so machinery and other essentials not available in Nigeria were obtained from Europe. Foreign nations were thus able to benefit from an agricultural development scheme in Nigeria.

The third demand by the World Bank was that the project, the recipient of substantial foreign funds, should be commercially viable. So far this has not been met, mainly because the smallholder aspect of the scheme has not been as successful as planned.

Operation of the Project

The role of Socfinco

Socfinco operates the plantation, which has progressed according to plan. Operations began in 1977–78 and in 1985 processed 75,300 tonnes of fruit. The oil yield was 10,860 tonnes and that of palm kernels was 4,392 tonnes. The estate now has two mills capable of processing 40 tonnes of fresh fruit bunches every hour. Nigerians are being trained for senior staff positions and for middle management. Some Nigerians were scheduled to take up senior management positions in 1986.

Rivers State and the smallholder unit

While the oil palm plantation is run by Socfinco, the smallholder unit was originally in the hands of Rivers State. The State's management of the Project has been weak. Lack of communication between the officials managing the scheme and the smallholders, and failure to keep up an adequate rate of funding, have further hindered the scheme. Cash flow problems have resulted. Smallholders have lost interest and many have remained subsistence farmers or simply stayed aloof from the Project. A parallel can be drawn with the Lafia ADP and with the irrigation projects of the north, where the systems failed as soon as bureaucrats had to communicate with smallholders or field level extension workers.

A parallel scheme to Risonpalm, Adapalm in Imo State, has avoided these problems because both the smallholder and plantation sections were controlled by the same management unit, in this case a foreign company. Such control may not always be successful or desirable but seems to have worked for the Adapalm scheme. Smallholders have been supplied with improved quality seedlings and fertiliser has been made available. A loan of 300 naira and a cash subsidy to cover costs of planting the new improved varieties have also been granted. Higher prices for oil palm fruit of a preferred type have encouraged smallholders to grow what the Company wanted, so production of oil from wild palms has gradually been giving way to a more modern type of production. The inputs were made available through a cooperative established specifically for this purpose. Farmers were able to repay loans through the cooperative, once they had been paid for their oil which was produced at Adapalm's own mills. There were many hitches in this system, not least dissatisfaction with the terms offered to smallholders by the company in charge. However, a significant element of mutual involvement was achieved in the first five years of Adapalm's life (1976–81), far more so than at Risonpalm. From 1986, however, Socfinco intended to control both the core plantation and the smallholder section at Risonpalm, thus reducing the involvement of Rivers State in the Project's management.

Smallholder development and Socfinco

In spite of the shortcomings of the smallholders' section of Risonpalm, Socfinco is indirectly encouraging smallholder production of palm oil. The company began collecting wild fruit growing around the estate. Socfinco guaranteed that it would buy any quantity of this wild fruit and would process it in the estate mills. The names of the suppliers together with the quantity of the fruit they had supplied were recorded, and a proportion of the mill's oil was made available to those particular smallholders at concessionary rates. The effects of this approach were largely beneficial:

1 trees in the wild that had long been neglected were now being 'rediscovered'. The bush surrounding them was cut back to allow the palms to grow and the crop was harvested.
2 if farmers had processed their own fruit, the oil yield would have been less than that extracted by the Risonpalm mill. The price paid for the fruit, together with the concessionary price of the mill's palm oil were together sufficiently attractive to discourage farmers from processing their own fruit. Selling to the plantation mill was, therefore, preferred and in 1985/86 over 50 per cent of the fresh fruit processed by Risonpalm was from the wild.

Yet another, though indirect, benefit was that smallholders had grown used to Risonpalm as a result of the wild fruit purchase scheme. They were no longer suspicious or hostile to its activities and this formed a firm foundation for Socfinco's intended takeover of the smallholder aspect of the scheme from Rivers State. As on the Adapalm project in Imo State, farmers were to be given financial incentives to plant varieties of oil palm preferred by the Risonpalm operators. They were also to be given other incentives to regenerate interest in oil palm production. With the relationship that had already developed with the smallholders, Socfinco were hopeful that the smallholder part of the scheme would progress rapidly.

Achievements and problems

The main achievement is that the Risonpalm plantation has encouraged the production of palm oil in Rivers State. Smallholders are increasingly being involved. The negative phase that tree crop farming went through during the petroleum boom is showing signs of bottoming out. However, palm oil produced by Nigeria is no longer for export but serves the growing domestic and industrial needs of her own population. In spite of attempts to increase production, the gap between supply and demand is not diminishing and by 1990 the shortfall is expected to be over 430,000 tonnes. According to *West Africa* (Nov. 25, 1985), there is virtually no realistic hope of Nigeria returning to its former export status. An investment of some 100 million naira per year would be required, coupled with the replanting of 20 to 30 thousand hectares of oil palms each year until the end of the century. The cost would be enormous and the necessary land is not readily available.

Problems on the Risonpalm Project range from ecological issues such as finding the most suitable varieties of oil palm for the region and the problems of preventing soil erosion, to financial and managerial issues. As in other large-scale projects such as the Lafia ADP (Chapter 5) there is a shortage of trained personnel. The same is true of other palm oil projects in the south. Trained personnel to work on the plantation or with smallholders are still in short supply. Substantial numbers of trainees pass through the project but many leave once their training is complete to find employment in the private sector. Until the early 1980s, the private sector had more to offer in terms of financial return than the public sector, under which agricultural development schemes fall.

Oil palm harvesting continues throughout the year, so, unlike field crops, there is demand for labour in most months, though peak demand is between March and May. Risonpalm employs over 2000 labourers, most of whom are employed on a casual basis. Payment is according to the nature of the tasks performed, which include:

1 harvesting
2 carrying the harvested product
3 cutting back the ground cover around the trees
4 working in the nursery to tend the seedlings
5 working in the maintenance workshops.

Although work is plentiful, the standard demanded by Risonpalm is high and workers have no form of job security. Union intervention is minimal and labour problems are common, as is conflict between Socfinco employees and plantation workers.

Summary

The question remains whether plantations such as Risonpalm (and there are increasing numbers of them in the south) bring greater benefits than costs. Clearly there are several issues involved.

Plantations, which are much more efficient than smallholders, undoubtedly have the potential to increase domestic production. However, management has to be efficient for the schemes to function well. As the plantations in Malaysia and Indonesia clearly revealed decades ago, managerial and political problems can reduce their efficiency levels to those achieved by smallholders.

By increasing the number of palm oil plantations, Nigeria is effectively consolidating land in the south into fewer hands. If such consolidation continues, landlessness could increase as land is obtained from projects such as Risonpalm by the Land Use Decree (Chapter 2). In Risonpalm's case, the state government implemented a type of 99-year lease, where each landholder is paid five naira per hectare per year, every five years. Most of the farmers from whom land was taken for Risonpalm's operation (mainly farmers with less than five hectares) now work for Risonpalm. The supply of rural labour could increase as a result of plantation schemes. This could present a conflict of interests to a government which is trying to increase domestic agricultural production and simultaneously support small farmers.

Assignments

Questions from A level examination papers

1 What measures have been taken to improve the productivity of farming in tropical areas? What have been the effects of such improvements? (Cambridge, June 1982)
2 Discuss the extent to which land reform leads to agricultural improvement. (London, June 1987)
3 (a) Describe and explain the difficulties faced by Nigeria in feeding its population.
(b) Discuss the ways in which the Government of Nigeria is attempting to increase food output. (Joint Matriculation Board, June 1982)

Conclusion

Drawing a conclusion on what has happened to agriculture in Nigeria since independence is difficult. We appear to be faced with a dilemma. On the one hand, there is the commonly held view, expanded in Chapters 1 and 2, that agriculture has declined in relative, if not in absolute, terms. On the other hand, the large number of development activities outlined at the end of Chapter 2 and detailed in the case studies in Chapters 4, 5 and 6 suggest some progress.

Nigeria's agricultural development programmes may have been extensive but their benefits to the rural sector have so far been minimal. The projects established during the 1970s, the heyday of oil, were not really a means of developing the rural sector but were show pieces. They were an attempt to show the world that Nigeria was a modern and developing nation with substantial resources which could pay for prestigious projects leading to instant development. The projects were also to satisfy international agencies such as the World Bank that foreign investments in Nigeria were being put to good use. Furthermore they were valuable in domestic politics. The urban areas had clearly been the recipients of most of the oil wealth and the rural areas had to be seen to be benefiting too. However, such projects are costly to operate.

Successive Nigerian governments showed less enthusiasm for running these prestigious schemes than they had for establshing them. The inevitable conclusion is that the schemes were never seriously seen as a means of improving the quality of life in the rural areas. If they had been, more attention would have been paid to their environmental and socioeconomic suitability.

While oil dominated the economy, the majority of Nigerians continued to depend directly on farming. In spite of this, agriculture has increasingly been looked upon as a backward and relatively unimportant sector. Once the oil started to flow, agriculture was no longer the main foreign exchange earner, nor was agricultural success so fundamental to the country's economy. Nigerians became used to the situation and in the midst of the oil boom, and even towards the end of it, there seemed to be little appreciation in Nigerian cities that the oil money might run out. At the time, Nigeria could afford all the imports she wanted, including foodstuffs, and there was no urgency to increase the productivity of the rural sector. Capital investment in agriculture may have been high in absolute terms but there was no real commitment to making the agricultural projects a success. With so much money available, developing the agricultural sector seemed at that time relatively unimportant.

Reality returned sharply with the end of the oil boom. The need for an efficient agricultural sector was once again apparent. In spite of all the adverse factors that have hindered its growth, agriculture has proved responsive to positive stimuli. In the short period since the Babangida regime assumed power, agricultural production has shown signs of increasing. If General Babangida adheres to his policies, the outlook for agriculture could be brighter than it has been since independence.

Recovery, however, will be a lengthy process. Even if the government does not waver from its determination to develop the rural sector and is not deposed, the availability of foreign investment could determine whether agriculture will advance. Also, two related factors suggest that Nigeria is unlikely to return to her former status as a major exporter of agricultural produce: the country's domestic market has grown and there is a new national determination to produce for the home market.

References

Abalu, G. O. I. and D'Silva, B. (February 1980), 'Nigeria's food situation problems and prospects', *Food Policy*, pp. 49–60

Adams, W. M. (1985), 'The downstream impact of dam construction: a case study from Nigeria', *Transactions of the Institute of British Geographers*, pp. 292–302

African Business (August 1986), 'Nigeria's economy "under the knife"', pp. 43–52

African Business (March 1987), 'Nigeria Survey', pp. 54–62

Andrae, G. and Beckman, B. (1985), *The Wheat Trap*, published by Zed Books, in association with the Scandinavian Institute of African Studies, Uppsala, Sweden

Areola, O., Faniran, A. and Akintola, O. (1985), 'The farmer-based small-farm schemes of the Ogun-Oshun River Basin Development Authority, South-western Nigeria', *Agricultural Systems*, 16, pp. 7–21

Bates, R. H. (1981), *Markets and States in Tropical Africa, The Political Basis of Agricultural Policies*, University of California Press, London, UK

Berry, S. S. (1975), *Cocoa, Custom and Socio-Economic Change in Rural Nigeria*, Oxford

Centre for Social and Economic Research (1979), 'Studies in a Town on the Kano River Project', report no. 3, Ahmadu Bello University, Zaria, Nigeria

Collier, P. (1983), 'Oil and inequality in rural Nigeria', in Dharam Ghai and Samur Radwan (eds), *Agrarian Policies and Rural Poverty in Africa*, ILO, Geneva, pp. 191–217

D'Silva, B. C. and Raza, M. R. (November 1980), 'Integrated rural development in Nigeria, The Funtua Project', *Food Policy*, pp. 282–297

Department of Rural Development, Federal Ministry of Agriculture, Agricultural Projects Monitoring, Evaluation and Planning Unit (March 1984), *Project Completion Report, Lafia ADP*, vol. 1, main report, Kaduna, Nigeria (J. Bivins)

Derrick, J. (December 1981), 'Decline of Agriculture shows no sign of slowing', *African Business*, p. 17

Economist Intelligence Unit (1986), 'Country Profile, Nigeria, 1986–87'

Folayan, A. (1983), *Agriculture and Economic Development in Nigeria*, Vantage Press Inc., New York, USA

Forrest, T. (1981), 'Agricultural policies in Nigeria, 1900–78', in Heyer, J., Roberts, P. and Williams, G. (eds), *Rural Development in Tropical Africa*, St Martin's Press, New York, USA

Green Paper on the State of the Nigerian Economy (1984), *Africa Development*, vol. 9, no. 3, pp. 116–161

Harrison Church, R. J. (1980 edition), *West Africa*, Longman, London

Hopkins, B. (1977), *Forest and Savanna*, Heinemann, London

Idachaba, F. S. (May 1985), *Priorities for Nigerian Agriculture in the Fifth National Development Plan 1986–90*, Federal Agricultural Coordinating Unit (FACU), paper, Ibadan

Kilby, P. (1969), *Industrialisation in an Open Economy: Nigeria 1945–1966*, Cambridge University Press, Cambridge

Kirk-Greene, A. and Rimmer, D. (1981), *Nigeria since 1970: A Political and Economic Outline*, Hodder and Stoughton, London

Longhurst, R. (1985), 'Cropping systems and household food security: evidence from three West African countries', *Food and Nutrition*, vol. 11, no. 2, pp. 10–16

Martin, S. (1987), 'Peasants, Planters and Mechanization: the oil palm industry in Eastern Nigeria', paper presented to the London Third World Economic History Group, 6th January 1987

Morgan, W. T. W. (1983), *Nigeria*, Longman, New York

Njoku, J. E. and Mijindad, N. B. (1985), 'The National Accelerated Food Production Project as a strategy for increased food production in Nigeria: a review of problems and prospects with particular reference to sorghum, millet and wheat', *Agricultural Administration*, vol. 18, pp. 175–85

Norman, D. W. (1982), *Farming Systems in the Nigerian Savanna — Research and Strategies for Development*, Westview Press Inc., Boulder, Colorado, USA

Oculi, O. (1979), 'Dependent Food Policy in Nigeria, 1975–79', *Review of African Political Economy*

Onyemelukwe, J. O. C. and Filani, M. O. (1983), *Economic Geography of West Africa*, Longman, New York

Richards, P. (1985), *Indigenous Agricultural Revolution*, Hutchinson, London

The Economist (3 May, 1986), 'After the Ball, a survey of Nigeria'

Udo, R. K. (1978), *A Comprehensive Geography of West Africa*, Ibadan

Usoro, E. (1974), *The Nigerian Oil Palm Industry (Government Policy and Export Production 1906-1965)*, Ibadan University Press, Ibadan

Wallace, T. (1981), 'The Kano River Project, Nigeria: the impact of an irrigation scheme on productivity and welfare', in Heyer, J., Roberts, P. and Williams, G. (eds), *Rural Development in Tropical Africa*, St Martin's Press, New York, USA

Wallace, T. (1981), 'The challenge of food. Nigeria's approach to agriculture, 1975-80', *Canadian Journal of African Studies*, vol. 15, no. 2, pp. 239-258

Wallace, T. (1981), 'Agricultural projects and land in northern Nigeria', *Review of African Political Economy*

Watts, M. J. and Bassett, T. J. (1984), 'Crisis and change in African agriculture: a comparative study of the Ivory Coast and Nigeria', *African Studies Review*, vol. 28, no. 4, pp. 3-27

West Africa (November 25, 1985), 'This is development', Nigerian agriculture 1, pp. 2465-67

World Bank (1986), *World Development Report 1986*, Washington

Index